Brian MacKay-Lyons

Tuns Press
Faculty of Architecture
Dalhousie University
P.O. Box 1000
Halifax, Nova Scotia
Canada B3J 2X4
URL: www.dal.ca/tunspress

General Editor: Essy Baniassad
Manager: Donald Westin

Distributed in the United Kingdom and Europe by:
Cardiff Academic Press, St. Fagans Road,
Fairwater, Cardiff CF5 3AE, United Kingdom

Brian MacKay-Lyons: Selected Projects 1986–1997
Editor: Brian Carter
Design: Brian MacKay-Lyons, Robert Meyer,
Susan Fitzgerald, Marc Cormier
Design Consultants & Typography:
Bhandari & Co.
Production: Donald Westin
Printing: Friesens

Canadian Cataloguing in Publication Data
MacKay-Lyons, Brian
        Brian MacKay-Lyons
        Includes bibliographical references
        ISBN 0-929112-39-3
1. MacKay-Lyons, Brian. 2. Architecture, Modern –
20th century – Nova Scotia. I. Carter, Brian, 1942-.
II. Title.

NA749.M33M33 1998   720'.92   C98-950028-4

Contents

Foreword

Essy Baniassad

The work of Brian MacKay-Lyons is some of the most original work in Canada currently. It is original in that it arises out of a close observation of ordinary buildings in the Maritimes, rather than from the conventions of a received vocabulary and aesthetic. It is radical in the context of what Brian MacKay-Lyons would regard as 'high brow' architecture because it does not draw on intermediate 'designed' models. It is at the same time conventional in the context of what he would call 'low brow' buildings in the vernacular tradition. Yet the work is quite consciously that of architecture as it embraces the history of architecture. It does so by drawing on the evolutionary process of that history – a process whereby form arises and is refined from earlier forms. Pevsner's duality doesn't apply to this work. There is a shed in the heart of every cathedral, a cathedral as the potential of every shed.

Each project in this book is particular to its program and place, each one a point in a continuous line of search and research in architectural design. As a collective body, the work is as rooted in the history of architecture as it is individually free from any one example of it, and embodies a morphology where the house is central to all forms.

Every form is, in an evolutionary sense, a development of the house. The schoolhouse, the courthouse, the house of worship, and many other references to public buildings as a 'house' suggest an attitude which underlies this work. And more importantly 'the house' offers the key to a question of how the present line of exploration would lead to designs in the architecture of the public domain.

The architects' minimal involvement in the architecture of the private dwelling today has created two fields out of one: housing as one; non-housing buildings as the other. It is surely axiomatic in architecture that the two complement and complete one another. They do so theoretically in terms of values and ideas, and actually, in the existence of the ultimate work of architecture – the city. In every period of history, ideas, metaphors and models draw upon some seminal idea, image or drive. The 'city', the 'church', the 'cathedral' and the 'house' have all served architecture. What form, what idea now serves architecture as such?

The house as the seminal idea underlying the unity of architecture has led to some bold attempts for the advancement of architecture. This axiom, left to the default in much of current practice and in many school programs, influences the work in this book. As such it serves the public as its primary cause, and advances architecture as a discipline beyond individual and particular instances. This book offers a record of a body of work that holds great promise of such a contribution.

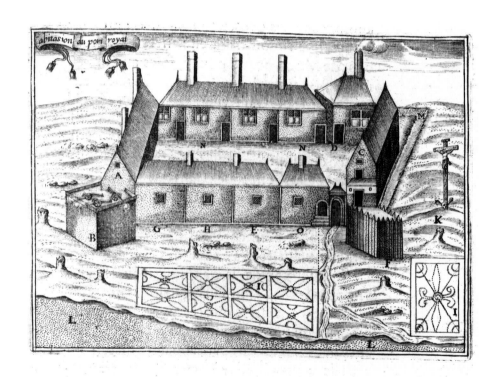

N ij

A Logemens des artifans.
B Plate forme où eſtoit le canon.
C Le magaſin.
D Logemét du ſieur de Pont-graué & Champlain.
E La forge.

F Paliſſade de pieux.
G Le four.
H La cuiſine.
O Petite maiſonnette où l'on retiroit les vtanſiles de nos barques; que de puis le ſieur de Poitrincourt fit

rebaſtir, & y logea le ſieur Boulay quand le ſieur du Pont s'en reuint en France.
P La porte de l'abitation.
Q Le cemetiere.
R La riuiere.

Sighting Land / Building at the Landfall

Brian Carter

Literature speaks the language of imagination,

and the study of literature is supposed to train

and improve the imagination. [1]

Northrop Frye

Nova Scotia, a narrow outcrop at the eastern edge of Canada with an extensive coastline forming a broad frontage to the Atlantic, has long been a landfall to the North America continent. When the adventurer Anthony Parkhurst counted 380 fishing vessels working the Grand Banks in 1578, he also noted that English, Spanish, French and Portuguese fishermen were trading with the aboriginal peoples, laying up stocks in the natural harbours of the Maritimes and moving into Atlantic Canada [2]. Twenty seven years later, Samuel de Champlain and the settlers of Acadia established l'Ordre du Bon Temps at Port-Royal. Organised to help entertain members of this isolated expatriate community during the long winters, this social club was founded a decade before colonists arrived in New England and almost two hundred years prior to the creation of Upper and Lower Canada.

Brian MacKay-Lyons was born in the village of Arcadia in the southwest of Nova Scotia. He grew up there and went on to study architecture in Halifax. In 1980, and after graduating, he left to enroll as a student of Charles Moore in the graduate program at UCLA. The architect of a series of houses, a member of the design team of Sea Ranch, respected teacher and the author of several important books, Moore saw architecture as the projection of human experience. As a consequence he spoke of how, in a discussion of architecture, one might usefully talk "about 'order' the way architects are endlessly doing" but also emphasise the importance of " 'reality' which architects almost never mention".[3]

MacKay-Lyons' return to Nova Scotia in 1983 was to a familiar reality. With an economy historically founded on shipbuilding and the seasonal fortunes of fishing and farming the austerity of life in the Maritimes is conspicuous. It translates into buildings which embody a distinct sense of order that can be readily identified in the vernacular of the cottage, shed and barn. The organisation of these buildings reflects basic needs and their construction an economy which is both essential and obvious. Rugged natural landscapes and the significant demands of climate together provide a physical setting for building which emphasises a stark reality at this particular place.

Like many young architects keen to build a practice, MacKay-Lyons became a designer of houses. In 1986, a radical and unsentimental transformation of a 200 year-old Cape Cod house on a bay at Kingsburg, transformed a series of small enclosed spaces into a single large two-storey high room with a new free-standing tower constructed at its centre. This tower – itself an emblematic hearth wrapped by a series of serviced inglenooks – offers both retreat and lookout. It also recalls Moore's formulation of "rooms to live in, machines that serve life, and the inhabitants' dreams made manifest". [4] The house makes further reference to Moore's work in its detail with large, stridently shaped cutouts in the walls of the tower, bright colours and simple forms which

< Habitation at Port-Royal: Samuel de Champlain
(Courtesy National Library of Canada)

'Ghost House', Upper Kingsburg, NS, 1994

give the project an almost toy-like quality. Planned for MacKay-Lyons' own family, this is a place where the dreams of the inhabitants have been very obviously made manifest.

Scrutinising the archetypal forms of the modest vernacular sheds of Nova Scotia and noting their relationships to site through a series of cognitive mappings of land, water and weather provided a basis for the development of MacKay-Lyons' work. The starkly simple envelopes, often focused around fireplaces and frequently distorted over time by the accretion of additional spaces, have provided inspiration. Aspects of similar indigenous buildings can also be readily identified in Moore's early work – houses which emphasised the large single volume, 'saddle bags' and the aedicule – and this congruity has helped to define a significant territory for architectural exploration which extends beyond the parochial.

Over a ten year period, MacKay-Lyons has used the designs for a series of houses in the Maritimes to interrogate the potential of modest means and to articulate a grammar of form and construction. That grammar has in turn provided a basis for the development of a language of spatial organisation. It is a language that is cognizant of the world yet inflected by the dialect of a particular place. So whilst the designs of earlier houses speak directly to a sense of order noted by Moore, and recall certain aspects of the work of Louis Kahn with its clear distinction of servant and served spaces, recent projects have also taken on an anthropomorphic quality. They are described by the architect in language that recognises the reality of a place where building and the provision of shelter are frequently just a necessity. For MacKay-Lyons these houses have 'bumps', 'sit' on 'dog-patch sites', turn their 'backs to the wind' and are constructed with a 'down-and-dirty, pay-as-you-go pragmatism'.

By combining teaching and practice in Nova Scotia, MacKay-Lyons has also sought to reveal the history of the place. That the many layered history of settlement, which has been so obviously shaped by geography at this threshold to the continent, can influence design and inform the act of building today is an important thesis. A series of design and build projects, directed by MacKay-Lyons and working with architecture students from the Technical University of Nova Scotia, has celebrated both the history and the dreams from hundreds of years of fitful occupation of this particular landfall. A series of Ghost Houses have been built upon the footings of buildings long gone. But, as a consequence of these projects, memories of these original buildings have been revived. Recognising the occupation of the place and the spirit of discovery, as well as the melancholy of failed human endeavour, these Ghost Houses are built in haste and with rudimentary systems constructed from materials readily at hand. They represent moments of intense inspiration, uncertainty, enthusiasm and ingenuity with an incendiary quality that vividly recalls the sighting of land and the first acts of settlement.

Nova Scotia vernacular outbuildings

As the designs for houses have developed many, like their indigenous counterparts, have acquired outbuildings. The stark singular envelopes of the Rubadoux/Cameron Studio and the Yaukey Cottage – or the Ghost Houses for that matter, have given way to the compositional groupings of the White/Leger House with a shed attached, the pairing of buildings for Fulcher/Sapos at Oxner's Head or the enclosing courtyard of House #12. Planning houses so as to make several buildings is a way of defining hierarchies of space. In an inclement climate it is also a move which allows houses to expand and contract with the seasons whilst creating valuable spaces in-between that help to adjust the micro-climate and establish places of habitation within a vast landscape.

The idea of the house as a group of buildings, like the Habitation at Port Royal in 1604-05, speaks of the need for self sufficiency in isolated rural settings. It also makes reference to the house as emblematic of the city. This aspect of the work of MacKay-Lyons is perhaps the most tantalising for, although the designer of houses for rural sites, he has simultaneously made opportunities to build in the city. Within an inner-city community in Halifax he has designed a series of urban buildings. The building on Creighton Street presents an investigation of the design of multiple housing within an established piece of urban fabric whilst the subsequent projects nearby on Maynard Street advance other ideas. The opportunity to initiate two projects on neighbouring sites prompted the investigation and testing of dense infill development, the incorporation of existing fragments of a city and the implications of planning for a mix of uses which support both living and work. Although the schemes import talismanic elements of rural life into the city – the canary yellow garden swing and solitary hut which appear almost surrealistically on a new constructed ground level high above the street – these buildings also defer to the pattern of the city. They convincingly rebuild streets, define public thresholds and create private spaces in ways which are frequently ignored by many modern developments that aspire instead to suburbanise the urban.

This interest in the reconstruction of the city through the addition of modest buildings has been expanded with the design of an extension to the School of Architecture in Halifax and a new building for Computer Science at Dalhousie University, these represent a different order of building. They are large, institutional and significant in their settings. The creation of a new room for the School of Architecture planned to house presentations and exhibitions which are open to the public is a manifestation of an idea of a school in the city. The design of such a building can, as Kahn suggested, be viewed as "the most honoured commission" [5] for an architect.

MacKay-Lyons' competition winning scheme was translated into a strikingly obvious metal shed attached to an imposing masonry building built in 1908 which housed the school in the

Snyder's Shipyard, Dayspring, NS

heart of the city. The form of this particular shed recalls places of fabrication and promotes a view of architecture that assertively connects design and construction. By contrast, the new Computer Science Building currently being designed for Dalhousie University occupies a prominent place on a discrete campus in Halifax. That design is in progress and consequently must await any detailed comment. Yet it clearly seeks to confirm the street and explore ideas of the public room first instigated in modest houses and subsequently developed at the School of Architecture in Halifax.

The design of this most recent building warrants new investigations of type. The project also brings with it a level of technical complexity which is of a different order than the previous work of MacKay-Lyons, and whilst the more recent designs for houses – like that for Fulcher / Sapos with its emphasis on the light envelope – underline a preoccupation with more refined expressions of construction, perhaps the tectonic form of this latest building will be inspired by different characteristics of the region. Might the design of houses illuminate investigations of other building types, materials and constructional systems? Can the shipbuilding traditions rooted in the construction of the Cape Islander and the Tancook Whaler be combined with more recent oil rig construction technologies that are now so obvious in the Maritimes? Will MacKay-Lyons be compelled to consider alternative manifestations of the vernacular and how might they inform the architecture of this building?

The questions which the design of this latest project begin to prompt also help to focus a view of the constructed work of MacKay-Lyons. It is work which has benefited significantly from a critical consideration of the order and reality that is embedded in the patterns of building at this particular landfall. It is work inspired by austerity and the overlap of construction, landscape and human occupation – work that is helping to train and improve the imagination in order to develop a meaningful architecture out of the most modest of means.

NOTES

[1] Northrop Frye, The Educated Imagination, CBC Publications, 1963, p. 57. Copyright 1963 by Northrop Frye. Reprinted courtesy of Stoddart Publishing Co. Limited, Canada; and Indiana University Press, 1964 edition.
[2] Jonathan Raban, Hunting Mister Heartbreak, Collins Harvill, l990, pp. 42-43.
[3] John W. Cook and Heinrich Klotz, Conversations with Architects, Praeger, 1973, p. 219.
[4] Charles Moore, Gerald Allen, Donlyn Lyndon, The Place of Houses, Holt, Rinehart & Winston, 1974, p. ix.
[5] Louis I. Kahn, Silence and Light, A+U, Vol. 3, No. 1, 13:01, p. 11.

Fulcher / Sapos House, Oxner's Head, NS

SELECTED PROJECTS 1986-1997

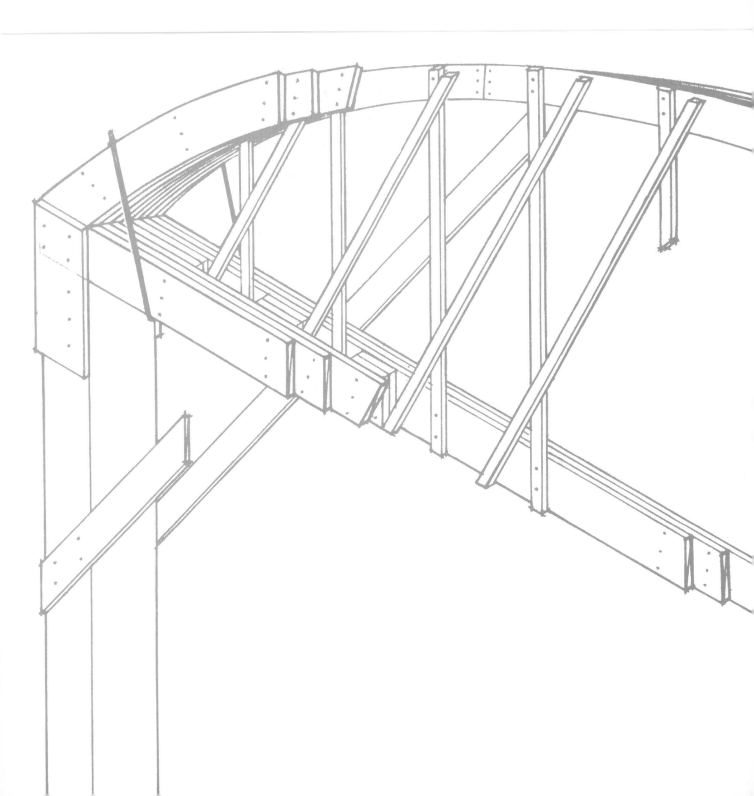

Modest Means

A bicycle shed is a building; Lincoln Cathedral is a piece of architecture. [1]

Nikolaus Pevsner

As a young student of architecture, I became suspicious of Pevsner's definition of architecture – it leaves much unexplained. After all, we know that symphonies have been inspired by folk dances; that literature has been derived from folk tales; that the great cuisines of the world have been born out of hardship; that the roots of Chicago jazz are in the Mississippi Delta blues; and that the culture produced in basements and garrets fills the great concert halls and art galleries. Yet, Pevsner's view remains the dominant tradition within our discipline.

The first six projects documented here have benefited from being small and inexpensive. They have necessitated pragmatism in order to be built. As a result, these projects come the closest to the 'zero' aesthetic of the vernacular buildings that I admire.

To the extent that there is an ideological basis for this type of work it is the conviction that architecture must be accessible. Henry Ford contributed to the democratization of technology by making an automobile that anyone could afford. I believe that the democratization of architecture is necessary to ensure its social relevance and the ultimate survival of the profession. Like the anthropologist who studies ordinary pots and pans, if one believes that culture derives from the everyday rather than the unique, then as a designer one is drawn to everyday things as a way of understanding the relationship between architecture and culture.

Limited budgets impose a design focus on building technology which is pragmatic rather than ideological. These projects are constructed of light timber framing due to the affordability of materials and labour, and compatibility with the climate of this region. In this regard, I have become interested in construction as a verb – a verb that describes a cultural process. This reflects an interest in primary construction rather than high craft as an end in itself and an enjoyment in watching the way that the various trades come to the site to create the layers of the composite building assembly. These projects employ a low-tech or 'folk-tech' approach to construction. They are, for the most part, within the vernacular material culture of the place that they sit.

Each of these modest projects has a counterpart in the body of work. However a small inexpensive project can focus on a single issue much like a research project in a test tube. It does not have the burden of complexity of larger and more expensive projects. In this way, these modest buildings provide the basis for the formulation of a grammar for the practice.

NOTES

[1] Nikolaus Pevsner, An Outline of European Architecture, 7th Edition, Penguin Books Ltd., 1963, p.15.

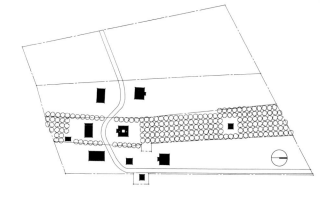

House on the Nova Scotia Coast #1

Upper Kingsburg, Nova Scotia, 1986

The concept for the renovation of a 200-year-old Cape Cod house in a village on the Nova Scotia coast was inspired by the stone foundations and central chimney masses which were the only remains of nearby burned farmhouses. This prompted the removal of the floors and walls of the original 13-room house.

In the design there is a contradiction between the two elements: perimeter 'house' and central 'chimney'. The perimeter is remade with traditional detailing and tiny Georgian windows contrasting the scale and the open plan interior with its modern 'chimney'.

The 'chimney' is a symbol for the centre of a world. It contains a new 5'-6" x 8'-0" stone fireplace, locally made wood stove, a bathroom, stair and ladder, closets, two bookcases, eight sleeping places, and a widow's walk.

The design integrates landscape, buildings, and furnishings. One hundred and fifty apple trees have been planted, to create a new 'orchard', which contains the buildings within a series of clearings.

This project is an essay on the special qualities of Nova Scotian vernacular architecture which refer to colour, skins, pragmatic forms and objects on the land. It is also an essay on archetypes recalling the hearth, house, grove and village. This underlines an understanding of the general through studying the particular, and seeing essential principles in ordinary things. When he was asked why he painted the hill at Kuerners in Pennsylvania so many times, the American painter, Andrew Wyeth, explained, "... I did want it to be all the hills, but yet a very definite hill." [1]

NOTES

[1] The Metropolitan Museum of Art, Two Worlds of Andrew Wyeth: Kuerners and Olsons, 1976, p. 101.

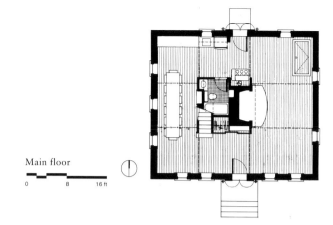

Main floor

0   8   16 ft

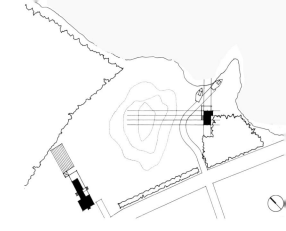

Rubadoux / Cameron Studio

Rose Bay, Nova Scotia, 1989

The 1200 ft.² artist's studio, constructed for $33,000 and designed with plans for phased development in the future, is stripped down both aesthetically and economically. It combines the vernacular precedents of the English barn and local fishing shed. The scheme also defers to the cultural landscape in its siting by occupying the least fertile edge of the site and consequently leaving the field untouched. In this regard, it is an environmental design project prompted by an architectural commission, which underlines an idea that the stewardship of the land is a prime responsibility of the architect.

The studio is a 25'-0" high primary volume which contains a loft, hearth/stair totem, and south-facing saddlebag. A virtual fourth bay, defined by the structural frame, extends the interior toward the sea. The northern corner of the structure is breached by two large, transomed glass doors which provide the maximum north light for painting. Giant sliding barn doors offer a controllable light shade.

The approach to the assembly of the structure is derived from an exploitation of the matter-of-fact sequence of building an apparently heavy timber frame from small, off-the-rack lumber pieces. In this regard, the project is informed by the resilient construction of the Cape Island boat used by the inshore fishermen of the area and the Snyder truss – a structural timber component developed by local boat-builder, Teddy Snyder.

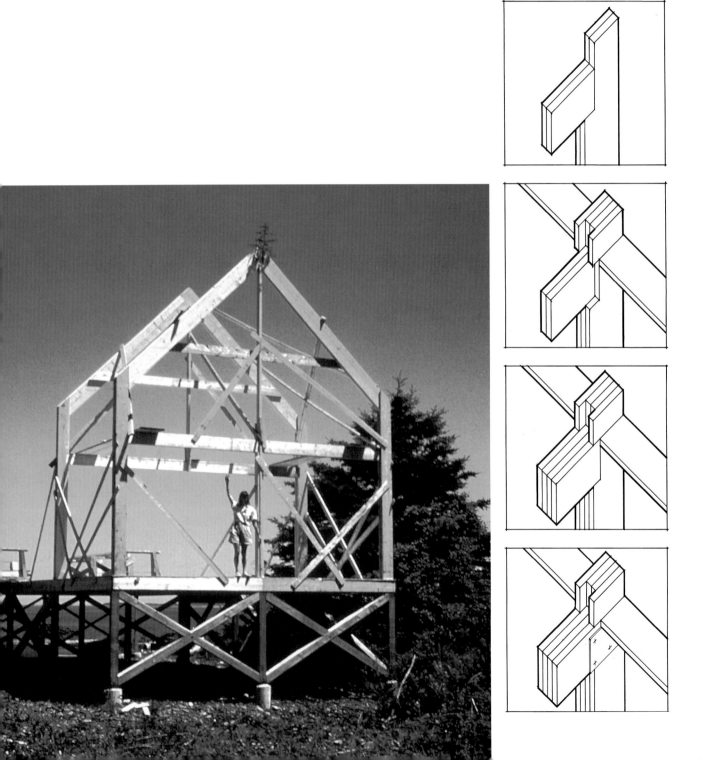

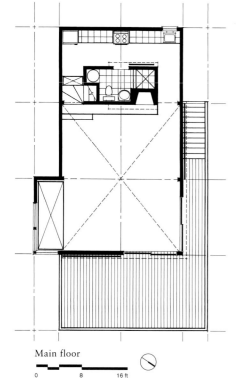

Main floor

0   8   16 ft

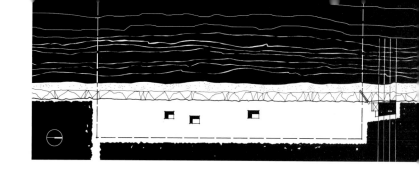

Yaukey Cottage

Blanche Peninsula, Nova Scotia, 1991

The Blanche Peninsula on the south coast of Nova Scotia is near Cape Sable Island, the heart of Maritime boat building traditions. The site is a remote, cliff edge meadow with foundation traces from an earlier settlement.

Tucked into the forest at the meadow edge, the building consists of a glass corner which faces both south and out to sea. In contrast, the north and forest facades are treated as an austere 'rump' of the building. A virtual fourth bay extends the plan southward, while a glazed saddlebag hangs over the edge of the cliff. Servant spaces are aligned on the forest side, protecting the served spaces and free-standing totemic elements, and foreshadowing the design of the later Leahey House.

This 1,300 ft^2 retirement home was built within a very constrained $55,000 budget to be fitted-out over time in the local pay-as-you-go tradition. An early experiment in prefabrication, the project was constructed of pre-cut components in just fourteen days, without electricity and in the dead of winter. Curved glue-laminated structural bents are infilled with platform framing and wrapped in a tight shingled skin. Interior finishes are limited to wood lath screens on the stair, hearth and barn doors. The result recalls the exposed wood framing of a boat.

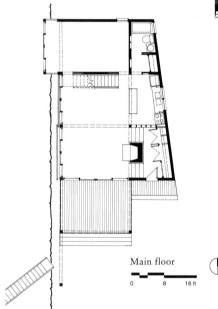

Main floor

0   8   16 ft

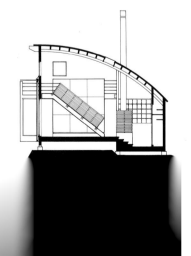

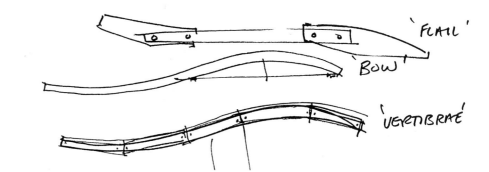

'FLAIL'

'BOW'

'VERTIBRAE'

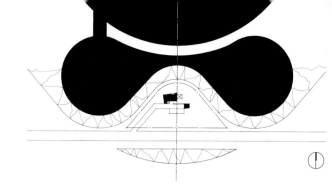

White / Leger House

Bayfield, Nova Scotia, 1994

The requirement was for a 1,600 ft^2 year-round home for a working couple with a budget of $85,000. Special needs included accommodations for yoga, a float tank, space for guests and a music room; a second phase provided a wood-shed. This is a house for Ceilidhs in a county known for its Celtic culture.

Situated on the agrarian north-facing coast of Nova Scotia, originally settled by Acadians and Highland Scots, the site is a small cres-cent-shaped cliff edge cut off by the road and overlooking a lagoon, a beach, and St. George's Bay. The bay is protected by two headlands: the eastern bluff supports a fishing port and the western bluff is occupied by a large dairy farm. The surrounding landscape is populated by simple, vernacular buildings clad in combi-nations of wood shingles and galvanized metal.

The scheme provides what is essentially a one room shed. It is a relaxed, distorted, primary form wrapped in galvalume and wood shingles inspired by the vernacular. An exposed portion of the building's basic platform construction signifies entry, especially when lit internally at night. This is echoed in the delaminated stick framing of the woodshed. The two structures sit in a pinwheel relationship to one another and are linked by a skeletal fence.

A great room is protected from the road by a box containing the servant spaces: kitchen, guest rooms, music box, storage, baths, a float room and space for yoga. One giant window from the great room looks out to sea, while another extends the space to the east toward the hilltop dairy buildings. A sleeping loft over-looks the great room.

A palette of familiar materials connects the project to its context and minimizes cost and maintenance. A galvalume, standing-seam roof folds down as an armoured wall which faces the sea and extends the cliff face, while the east, south and west walls are wrapped in cedar shingles. The main floor and terrace extension are polished concrete slab-on-grade. The slab contains an in-floor hydronic heating system driven by a conventional hot water heater and boosted by a wood stove. During storms on this windswept shore, or when the owners are travelling, cedar barn doors make it possible to close up the house.

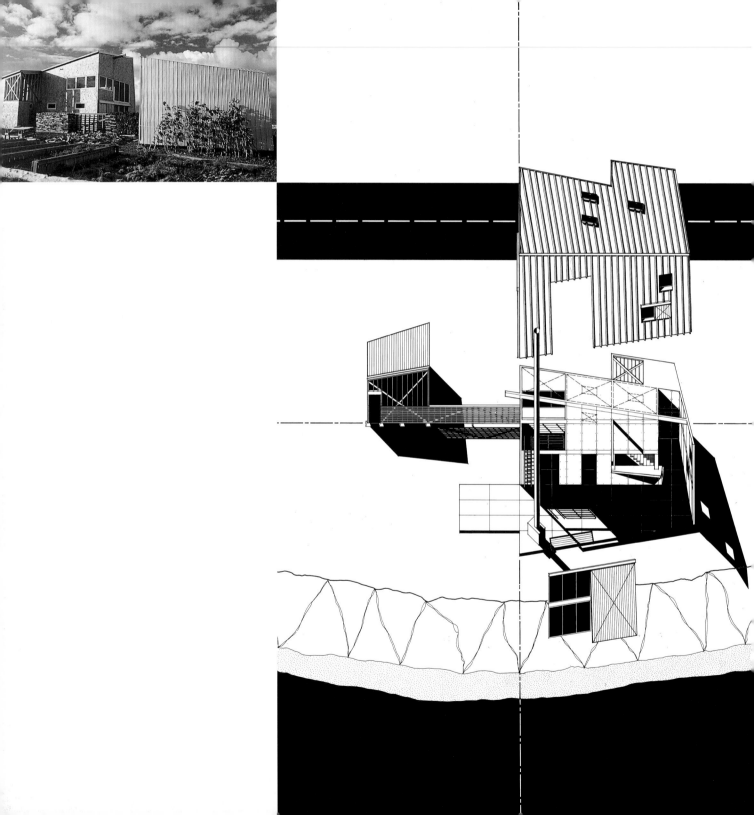

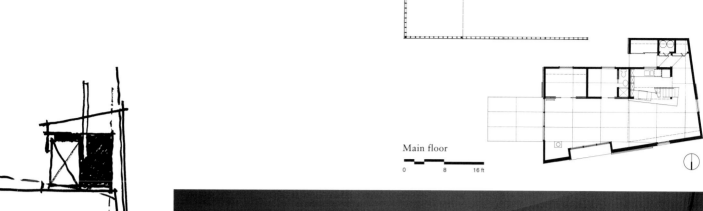

Main floor

0   8   16 ft

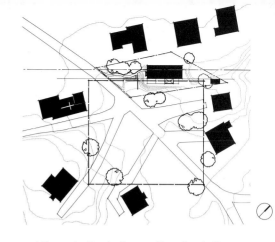

Messenger House

Halifax, Nova Scotia, 1997

This 1200 ft² house for a couple is located in Halifax. The neighbourhood's mix of rural cottages, bungalows, vegetable gardens and upscale new houses is messy evidence of a living culture.

The site is a rhombus-shaped plot between back yards. By turning the house, the primary facade is able to combine with borrowed front lawns, the road and a tiny Baptist church to formalize the reading of a 'village green'.

The entrance into the house is through a narrow, glazed space between the hearth and a large bookcase. The bookcase is the back of this archetypal lean-to form which contrasts with the totally glazed south front.

A protruding bathroom separates the public from the more private terraces outside, as well as providing an elevated second level balcony with a view over the 'village green'. The bathroom, together with the kitchen, laundry, storage and mechanical room, are condensed into a core which acts as a threshold between the public and private ends of the house. A loft forms a 'lid' over the core and downstairs bedroom.

This house consists of two parts. The first incorporates the grounded elements – heated concrete slab, bookcase, foundation wall, hearth and the projecting bathroom. The other is the zero-detailed, shingled box above. Glazing is treated as a continuous void between, as if formed by one continuous cut into the shingled box. Both inside and outside the 'framing' is expressed where revealed by glazing.

The creation of a single material skin and, in particular, wood shingles, is a response to the logic imposed by an extremely labile climate and the region's material culture. The triple layers of shingles with woven corners respond to the wet-dry, freeze-thaw cycles like the feathers of waterfowl and explain why wood structures in Atlantic Canada can last hundreds of years.

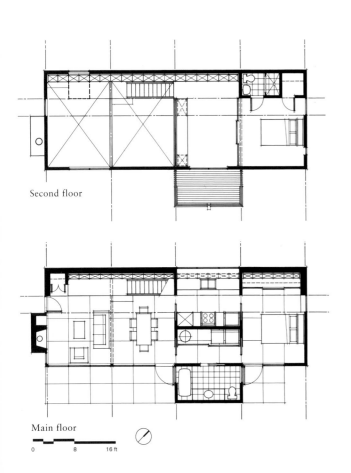

Second floor

Main floor

0   8   16 ft

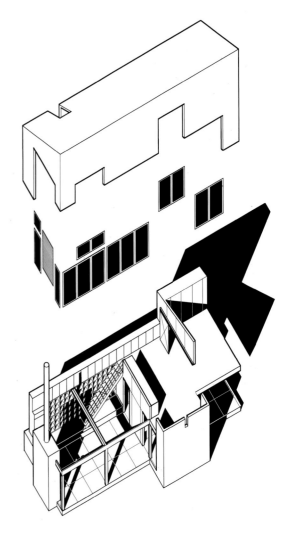

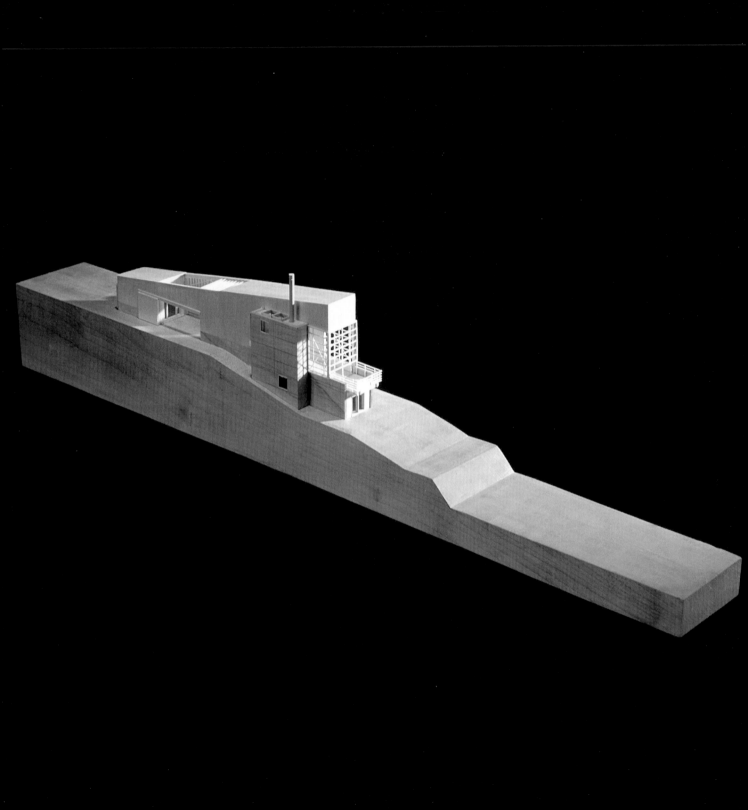

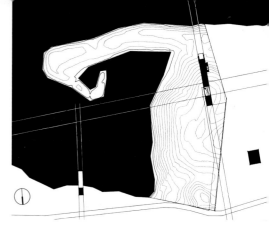

Howard House

West Pennant, Nova Scotia, 1995

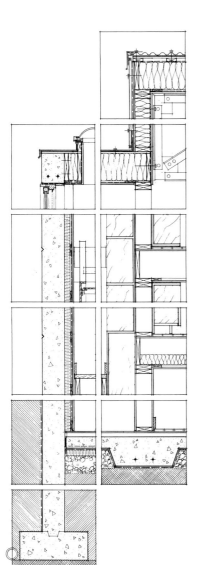

The house of about 2,000 ft.^{2}, designed for a young family, is an example of an affordable metal box. It represents the findings from a particular avenue of design research .

The house creates a 12'-0" wide, 110'-0" long wall in the landscape. Built on a four acre field surrounded by the sea on three sides, there is a domesticated fishing cove to the east, with wild, open sea to the west. To the south is the shore of a bay. The rough-and-ready wrapper of the house is in keeping with the 'dog-patch' setting. The exterior skin is standard, industrial, corrugated galvalume. The raised top-of-concrete line of the foundation celebrates the relative difficulty involved in getting buildings out of the ground in a cold weather climate. A heavy, concrete stair bump is a protective gesture providing shelter from the prevailing westerly winds off the open sea.

A monolithic, monopitched shed roof climbs to the south covering one continuous, unobstructed living space. It extends from the garage, to the entry court, over the kitchen and living room to a cantilevered deck. This tube is punctuated by several totemic elements which inflect it. The bridge, a well, the hearth and a south-facing window provide a distinct series of places within the house. The spatial reading of the tube is further emphasised by a trough of hardwood flooring that turns up the walls of the elevated concrete foundation making a wainscoting sill in the main living area. Three bedrooms have been planned at the lower level, while a master bedroom/study occupies a second floor loft. Delaminated walls and ceiling expose conventional platform framing.

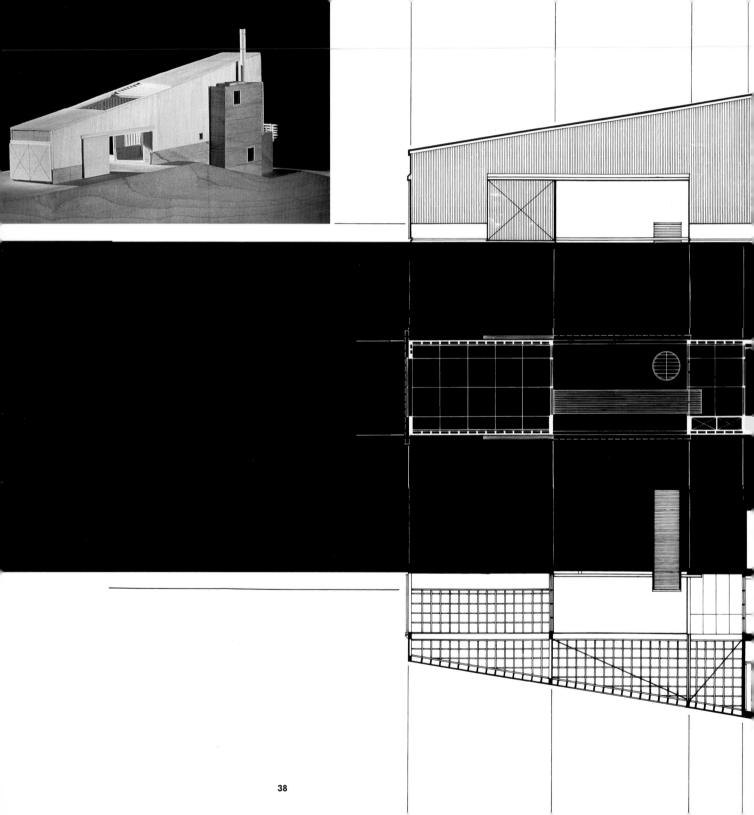

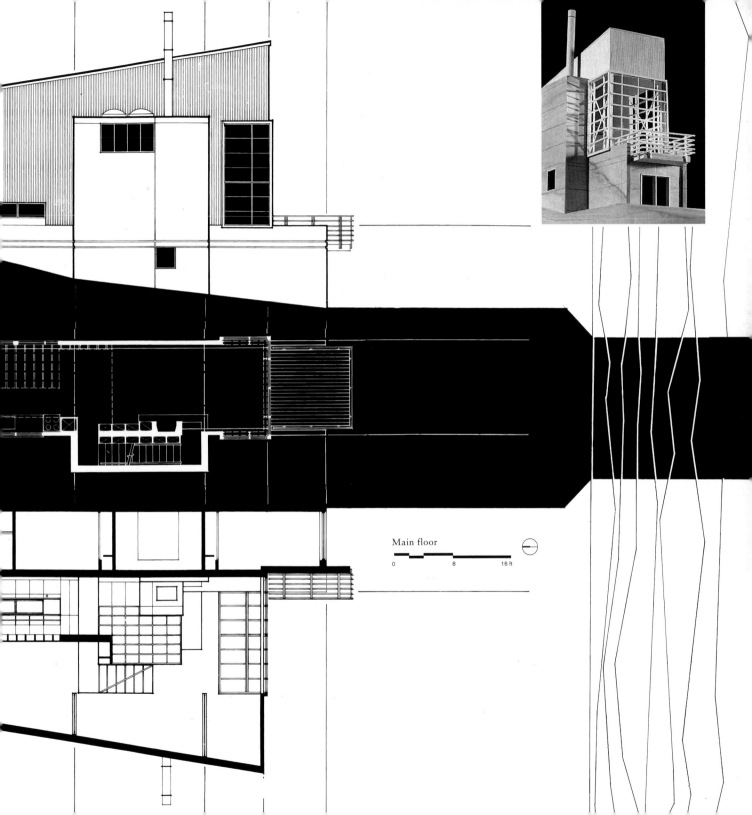

Main floor

0   8   16 ft

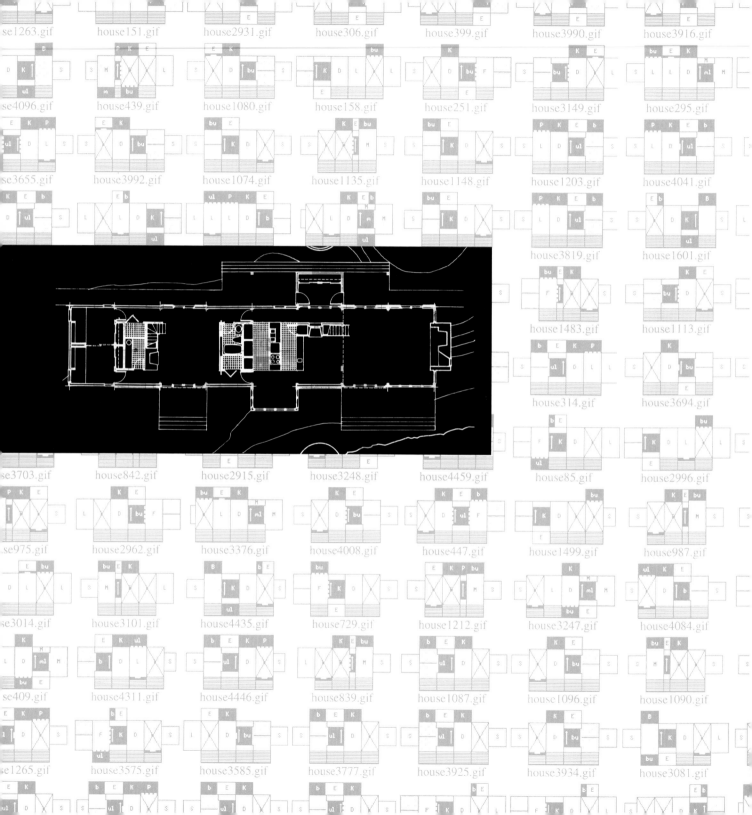

se1263.gif   house151.gif   house2931.gif   house306.gif   house399.gif   house3990.gif   house3916.gif

se4096.gif   house439.gif   house1080.gif   house158.gif   house251.gif   house3149.gif   house295.gif

se3655.gif   house3992.gif   house1074.gif   house1135.gif   house1148.gif   house1203.gif   house4041.gif

house3819.gif   house1601.gif

house1483.gif   house1113.gif

house314.gif   house3694.gif

se3703.gif   house842.gif   house2915.gif   house3248.gif   house4459.gif   house85.gif   house2996.gif

se975.gif   house2962.gif   house3376.gif   house4008.gif   house447.gif   house1499.gif   house987.gif

se3014.gif   house3101.gif   house4435.gif   house729.gif   house1212.gif   house3247.gif   house4084.gif

se409.gif   house4311.gif   house4446.gif   house839.gif   house1087.gif   house1096.gif   house1090.gif

se1265.gif   house3575.gif   house3585.gif   house3777.gif   house3925.gif   house3934.gif   house3081.gif

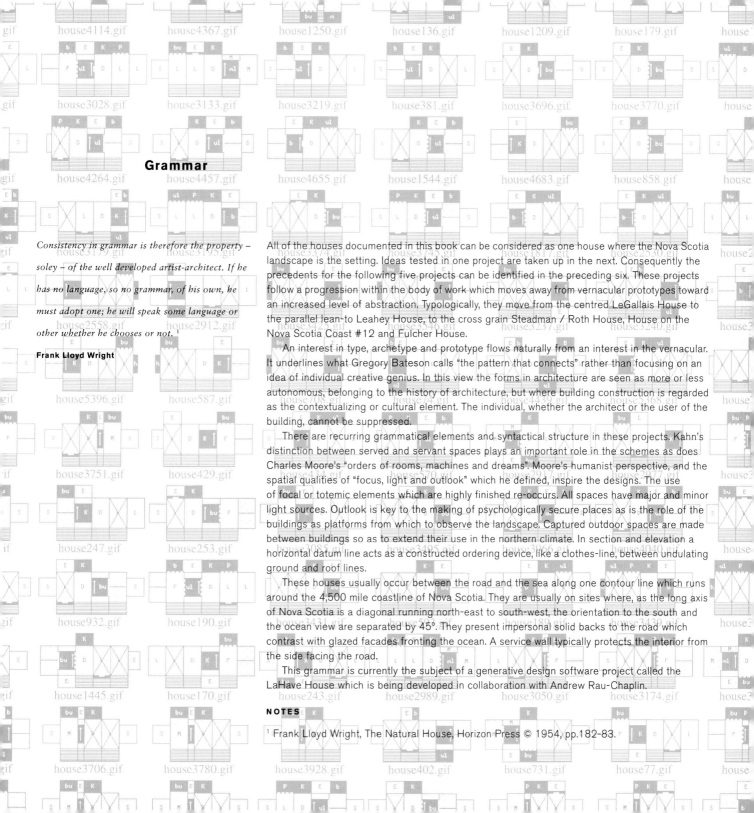

Grammar

*Consistency in grammar is therefore the property –
soley – of the well developed artist-architect. If he
has no language, so no grammar, of his own, he
must adopt one; he will speak some language or
other whether he chooses or not.* [1]

Frank Lloyd Wright

All of the houses documented in this book can be considered as one house where the Nova Scotia landscape is the setting. Ideas tested in one project are taken up in the next. Consequently the precedents for the following five projects can be identified in the preceding six. These projects follow a progression within the body of work which moves away from vernacular prototypes toward an increased level of abstraction. Typologically, they move from the centred LeGallais House to the parallel lean-to Leahey House, to the cross grain Steadman / Roth House, House on the Nova Scotia Coast #12 and Fulcher House.

An interest in type, archetype and prototype flows naturally from an interest in the vernacular. It underlines what Gregory Bateson calls "the pattern that connects" rather than focusing on an idea of individual creative genius. In this view the forms in architecture are seen as more or less autonomous, belonging to the history of architecture, but where building construction is regarded as the contextualizing or cultural element. The individual, whether the architect or the user of the building, cannot be suppressed.

There are recurring grammatical elements and syntactical structure in these projects. Kahn's distinction between served and servant spaces plays an important role in the schemes as does Charles Moore's "orders of rooms, machines and dreams". Moore's humanist perspective, and the spatial qualities of "focus, light and outlook" which he defined, inspire the designs. The use of focal or totemic elements which are highly finished re-occurs. All spaces have major and minor light sources. Outlook is key to the making of psychologically secure places as is the role of the buildings as platforms from which to observe the landscape. Captured outdoor spaces are made between buildings so as to extend their use in the northern climate. In section and elevation a horizontal datum line acts as a constructed ordering device, like a clothes-line, between undulating ground and roof lines.

These houses usually occur between the road and the sea along one contour line which runs around the 4,500 mile coastline of Nova Scotia. They are usually on sites where, as the long axis of Nova Scotia is a diagonal running north-east to south-west, the orientation to the south and the ocean view are separated by 45°. They present impersonal solid backs to the road which contrast with glazed facades fronting the ocean. A service wall typically protects the interior from the side facing the road.

This grammar is currently the subject of a generative design software project called the LaHave House which is being developed in collaboration with Andrew Rau-Chaplin.

NOTES

[1] Frank Lloyd Wright, The Natural House, Horizon Press © 1954, pp.182-83.

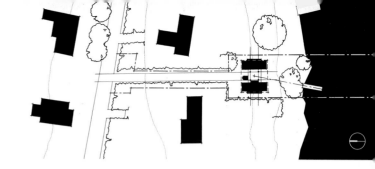

LeGallais House

Bedford, Nova Scotia, 1992

A permanent residence for a young family sited on the shore of Bedford Basin in the inner chamber of Halifax Harbour. This community, consisting of old farmhouses, former cottages, new suburban homes and strip commercial development, has been absorbed into the metropolitan area of the City of Halifax. The new lot was created from a wooded fringe between two existing homes.

The straightforward English barn form is built to setback lines and pulled forward from its neighbours to create the impression of an old outbuilding. The axis created by the long driveway approach extends through the transparent living room and out to the water. The servant spaces of the house are planned to present a solid massing to the road and the building is expressed as a gabled roof floating on a clerestory over solid blocks. In contrast on the water side it is deconstructed. It contains the served spaces and is expressed as a gabled roof floating over external terraces. As with several of the other houses, the denser servant spaces or 'machines' protect the interior 'rooms' both from the road and at the side yards by the addition of 'blinder' saddlebags. The parti, which recalls the English barn, consists of a 35'-0" high central living area – the 'threshing floor', that is flanked on either sides by 'stables' containing kitchen and garage, and corresponding 'hay lofts' above for second and third storey bedrooms. A two-way tartan grid provides a clear circulation zone.

The exterior consists of a tight skin of eastern cedar shingles. The interior offered an opportunity to develop a palette of wood finishes, ranging from a rustic cedar telephone pole aedicule, to planed and rough sawn exposed framing, a maple plank bridge and raised hearth. Extensive use of miscellaneous metal elements resolve the connections structurally and formally between wood elements. The structure was designed to provide its own scaffolding, with two side blocks and the aedicule supporting the floating roof. This cedar aedicule marks the centre of the world for the inhabitants while formalizing the cedar, tree-lined driveway axis.

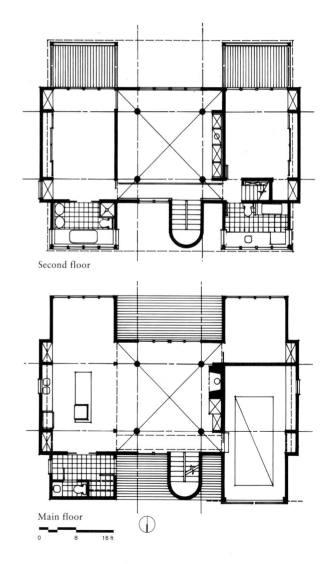

Second floor

Main floor

0   8   16 ft

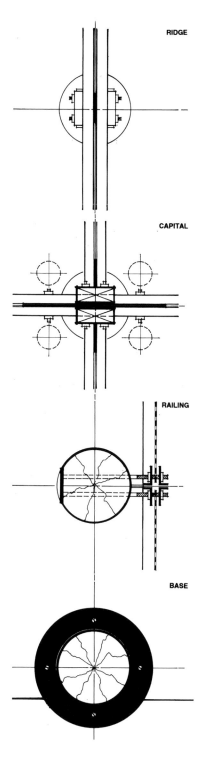

RIDGE

CAPITAL

RAILING

BASE

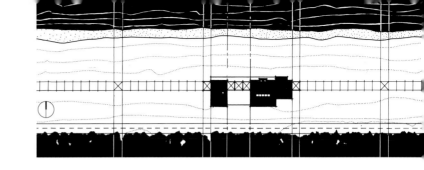

Leahey House

Pugwash, Nova Scotia, 1994

The house provides 3,400 ft² of enclosed space and is designed to be enlarged. Beginning as a two bedroom vacation home with a detached shed, a second phase, currently in design, will transform the shed into a larger two bedroom guest house and plan for the addition of a detached pavilion. Consistent with this plan for incremental growth, new furniture and specially designed fittings are being added annually. Ultimately the house will become a permanent home for the clients when they retire.

Nova Scotia's 4,500 mile long coastline consists of distinctly different cultural landscapes. The house is located on the north-facing Northumberland Shore, on a cultivated coastline strip which rolls gently down to the sea. Each original land grant settled by Scots is a strip bordered by hedgerows containing forest, road, field and beach. Long, thin, silver-roofed barns that lie parallel to the shore form a recurring 'back beat' as one drives through this landscape. The main building and shed are pulled apart to form a sunny deck and frame views of the ocean on arrival at the site. These spaces also help to create micro-climates which extend the use of outdoor spaces in the north. The building divides the site, forming a garden court on the road side and retaining a large field on the water side.

The scheme is composed of three principle tectonic elements: frame, roof and totems. The post-and-beam frame – a structure in the landscape that provides for growth – recalls the long timber barns of the region. The standing seam galvalume roof is slung over portions of the frame to provide an archetypal, lean-to shelter. The bay window, hearth, stair, library and a kitchen island are designed as totemic elements which stand beside the frame, domesticating the scheme, and providing comfort and amenity.

The design grammar is articulated in the zoning of the house into what Charles Moore calls "the order of rooms" versus "the order of machines'" This spatial strategy is given further expression in this house by the contrast between platform framing and heavy timber framing. The served 'rooms' are constructed of freestanding heavy timber which is designed to carry gravity or vertical loads. The servant 'machines' are constructed of platform framing which lends itself to resistance to horizontal wind loads. Plywood clad fins or box trusses transfer horizontal and vertical load components into the respective framing systems below and ultimately onto the foundations.

The Leahey House has emerged as a clear example of a coast house morphological type – a sheltered viewing platform parallel to the sea.

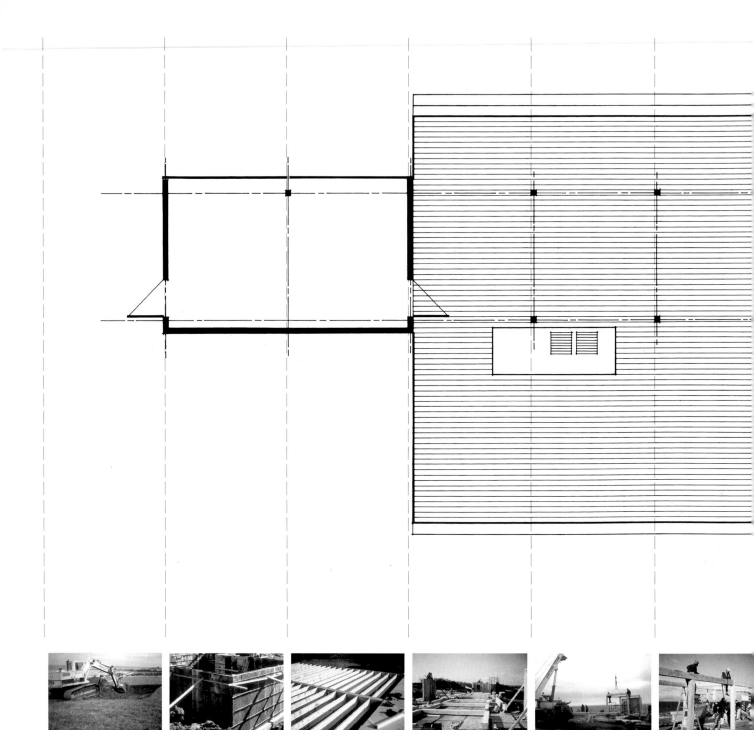

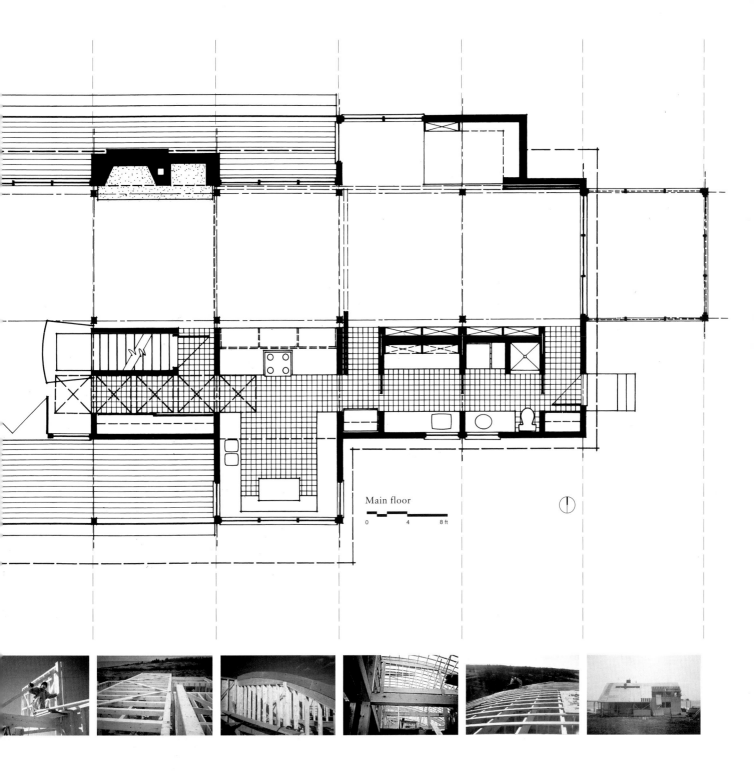

Main floor

0   4   8 ft

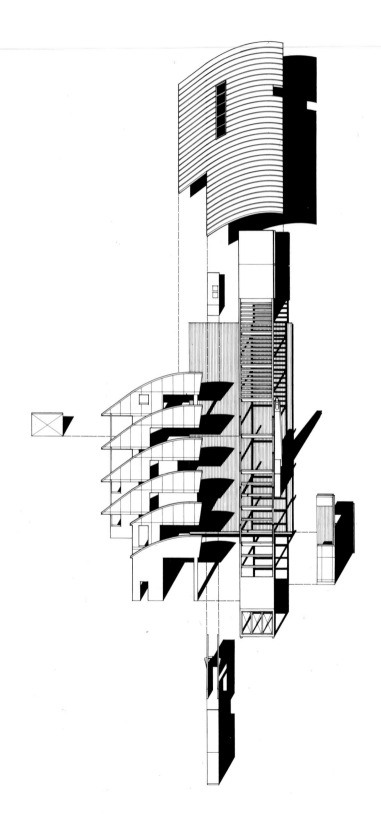

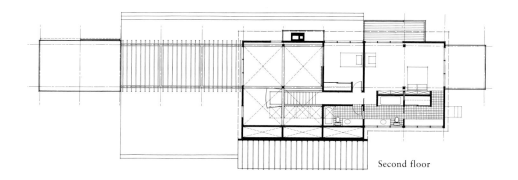

Second floor

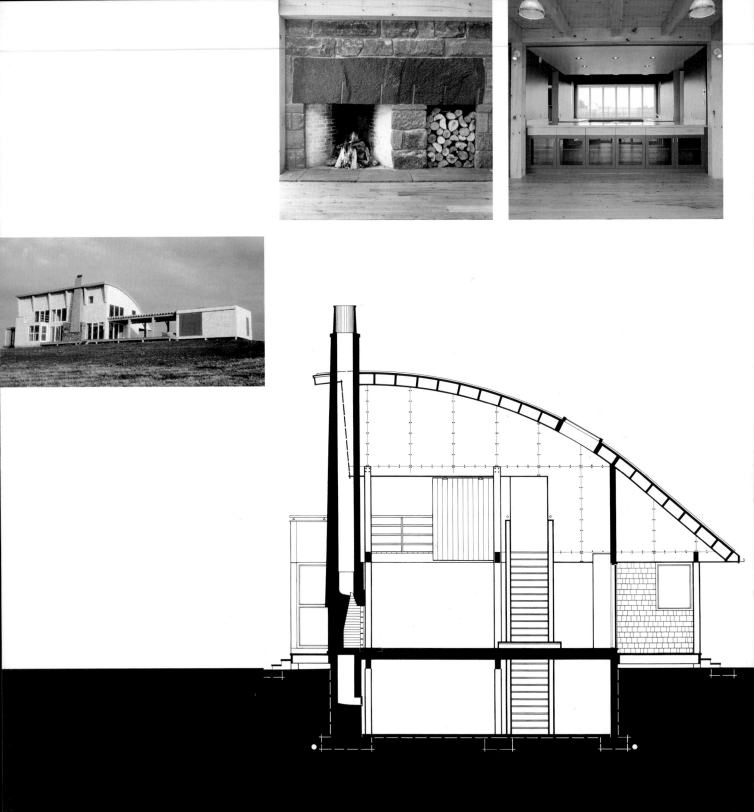

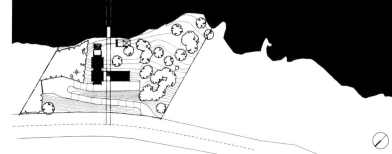

House on the Nova Scotia Coast #12

South Shore of Nova Scotia, 1996

The house consists of two principal elements which form a southeast orientated courtyard. The garage acts as a mute retaining wall parallel to the road, while the living spaces are contained in a cross-slope pavilion. The road side face contrasts with the private sea side of the site. The standing seam galvalume roof folds down on the street facade as a protective gesture, while the house extends to the water on the sea side, with large windows and a deck. Approaching from the road there is a view over the roof to the sea. A strong visual axis passes through a porch to an existing wharf. The porch, with its exposed construction, celebrates the entry to the site and building.

The plan and section of this year-round home create a wide-open public level with secondary private spaces tucked under, and the main bedroom suite and study in a mezzanine above. A 'great room' is contained within a 16'-0" wide hollow tube which projects out to sea. It is served by four flanking servant bays, one of which is extruded to become the garage.

Moving through the great room toward the sea creates a procession through spaces alternately protected by flanking bays then open glazed voids. The two bays on the north side of the plan are dense, while the two bays on the south and east sides are bright and open.

The passage through the house is punctuated by a series of totemic elements. Upon entering, one is aligned with a kitchen island as a foreground element to the working kitchen, contained within one of the flanking bays.

Beyond the dining area one enters the double height sunken living area punctuated by the hearth, bookcase and a hidden stair. A two-storey glass bay creates an added zone to the living space and the outdoor deck extends the house to the sea.

The construction strategy for the building begins with a concrete base which transforms the sixty foot slope across the site into a series of terraces to receive the stick-framed pavilion. The top-of-concrete line through the great room acts as a horizontal datum which is above the floor between the sloped ground line and the opposing slope of the roof line.

This concrete base, together with four timber frames, form the primary structure for the house. The structure is largely a response to lateral wind loads given the exaggerated height and narrow width of the building. The four wind shear frames form rigid rings which wrap around the great room. They consist of concrete grade beams at the bottom, rustic wind trusses above and plywood buttresses at the sides.

The primary structure is completely wrapped by the flush zero-detailed, shingled envelope creating a northern climate relationship between structure and envelope that differs from the usual warm climate modernist approach. In section, the envelope consists of an outer metal roof skin with a corresponding plywood interior liner and an interstitial space with services and lighting.

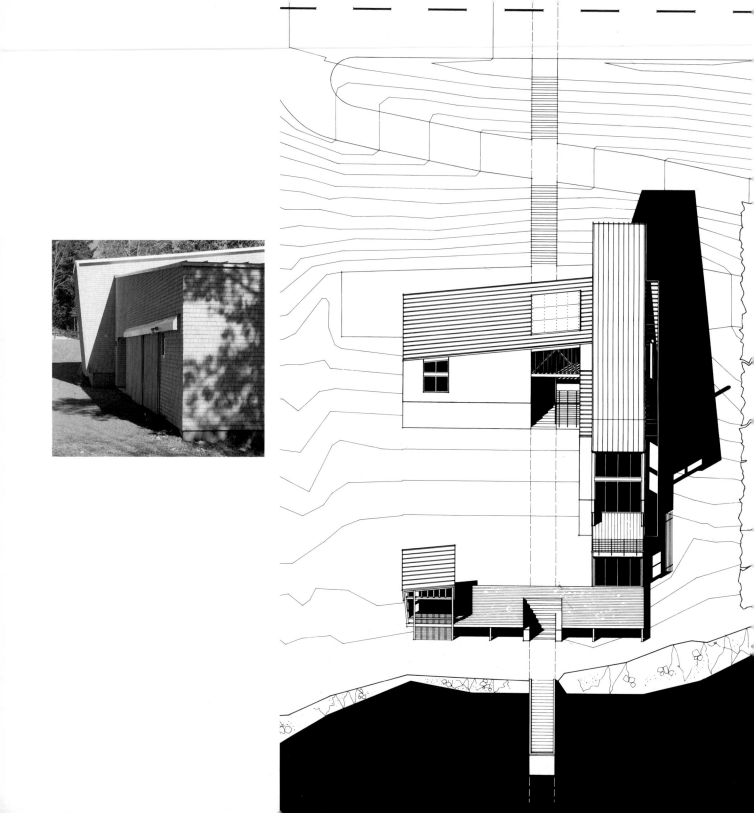

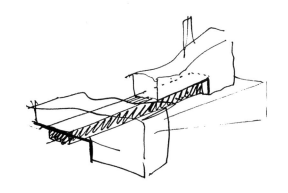

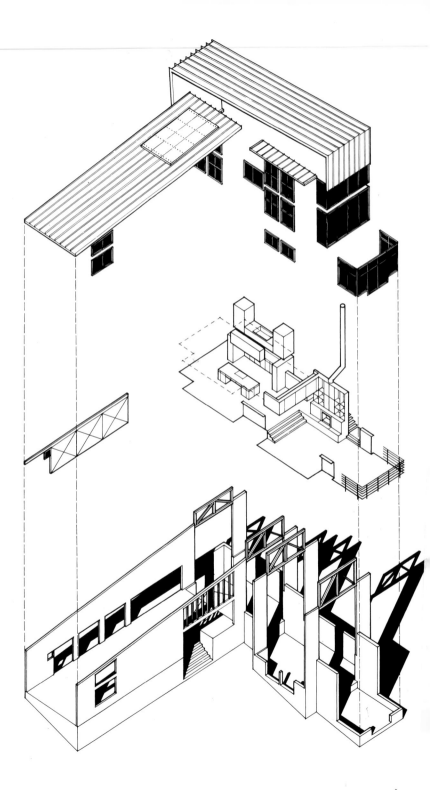

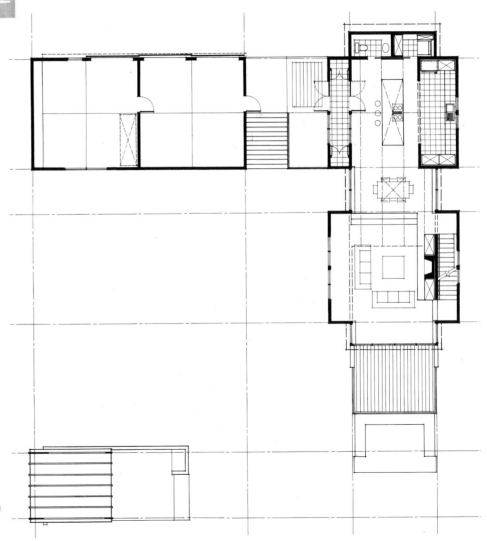

Main floor

0   8   16 ft

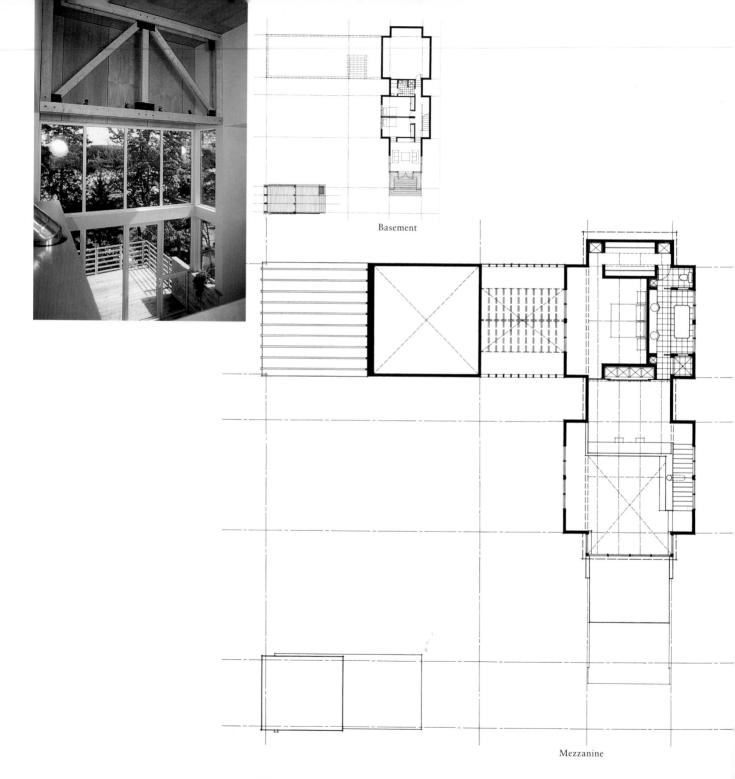

Basement

Mezzanine

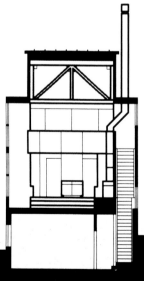

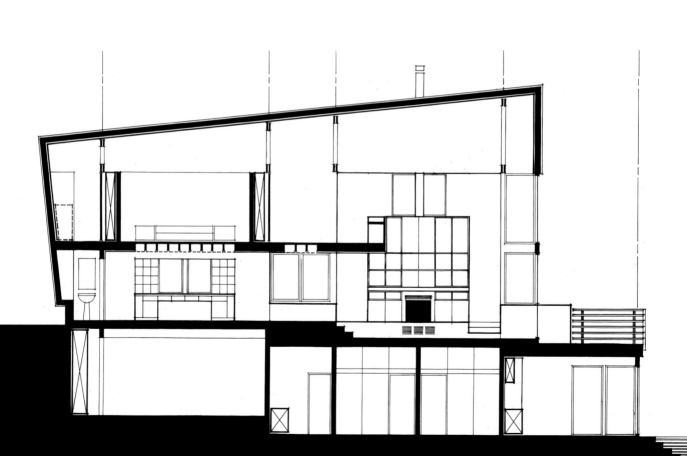

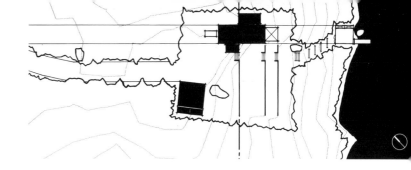

Steadman / Roth House

Cambrian Cove, Nova Scotia, 1997

This small house for a professional couple is perched above a lake in a glaciated landscape covered with hardwood forest and littered with boulders. The approach axis is framed between the house and the garage, and the path continues down to the lake and the dock. The entry to the site is formal and direct while the entrance into the house is indirect and less obvious.

The pinwheel relationship between the articulated house form and the mute garage provides semi-protected courtyards. These embrace the forest landscape and create microclimates, extending the use of the outdoor space. Likewise, alternating large glazed areas draw the forest to the inside. The long axis of the house looks south-east down the long axis of the lake.

At a formal level, this house is essentially a box articulated by hovering, boxlike projections. The double height great room contains the served spaces and the projecting bays contain the servant spaces – the entry, kitchen, storage, bathrooms, study and a porch. In the section of this house the lesser rooms are tucked under in a concrete base and the main bedroom is designed as a suspended loft in the great room.

The construction is platform framing. The structure deals with the desire for open, double-height interior space by transferring wind shear loads through the envelope like a torsion box.

In addition, the projecting bays act as wind shear buttresses, huddling around the great room.

The roof-ceiling structure extends this platform framing language. Its double 2"x10" at 24" on centre roof joists create a scissors effect with a concave wood ceiling. Its undulating geometry is derived from the need for roof drainage which culminates in a giant galvanized scupper that pours into a fountain.

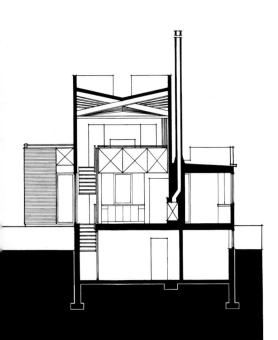

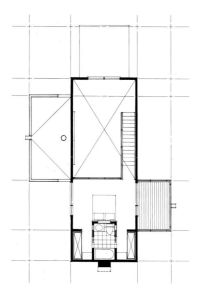

Loft

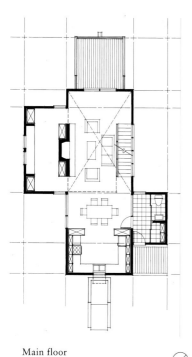

Main floor

0   8   16 ft

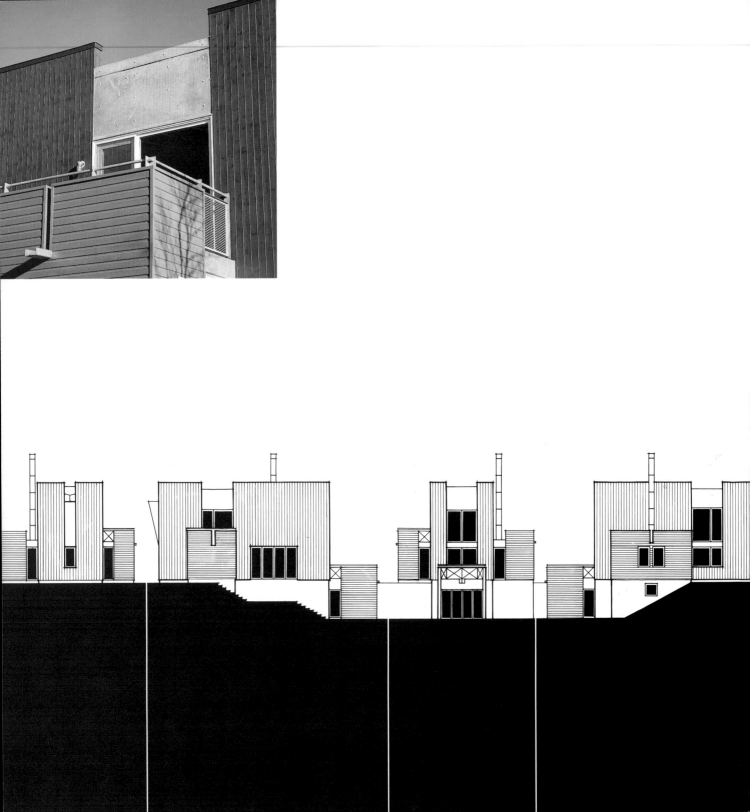

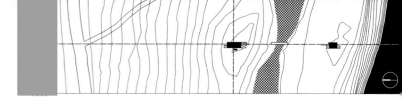

Fulcher / Sapos House

Oxner's Head, Nova Scotia, 1997

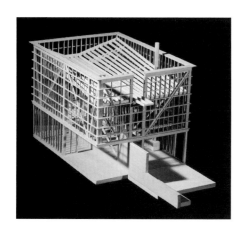

This house is located at the point where the LaHave River meets the sea. A pair of lantern-like buildings appear to float above two hilltops; one overlooks the river estuary and the other the ocean; one contains the main house and the other the guest house. These two structures each sit on drumlins and are aligned on a north-south axis. The natural wetland formed between the drumlins is embraced as a 'central garden' and a wildlife corridor through the site. The mirrored major and minor buildings are separated by approximately 450 feet, but are linked by concrete block walls which gesture toward the garden. A horizontal datum at 8'-0" above the main floors ties the two together as an absolute man-made ordering device playing against the undulating natural topography. On entering the cove, the building presents a concrete block hearth which is designed as a totem at the scale of the landscape. Climbing up to the building, two glowing entry porches are revealed.

In each building the entry and servant elements are organized on the east side of the concrete wall. The served space, within the free plan, creates the feeling of an infinitely long great room. An 8'-0" high 'belt' of glazing and horizontal sliding barn doors forms the base of the building while the second floor appears to float above as an inhabited, truss-filled box. The ground floor receives its natural light from a wraparound glass belt. By contrast, the 'attic' story is lit by a repetitive field of windows which are punched into the floating wood box. The sole totemic element within the building is a plinth. It articulates the long block wall creating a kitchen island, a stair, a desk, a seat, and finally a scupper/fountain pouring water from the roof out toward the wetland garden.

The scheme consists of two archetypal material systems. The first are the heavy, grounded, concrete elements – a heated floor slab, block wall and the block hearth. The other consists of the wood framed elements floating above the ground. The finger-jointed, folk-tech timber frame is completely visible on the inside, channelling much of the horizontal and vertical loading into the centre of the plan, and emphasizing the distinction between frame and envelope. The rough-sawn, channel-joint hemlock envelope is a rain-screen wrapper protecting the structure. Sliding barn door tracks, concealed in the rain screen cavity, allow giant, flush metal barn doors to transform the house from a mute box closed against the weather to an open pavilion.

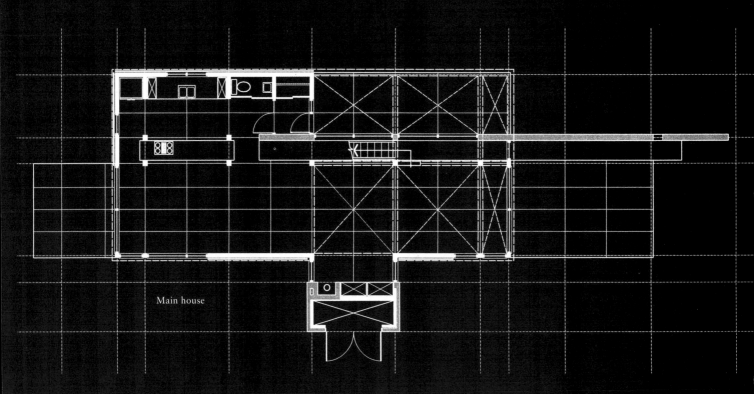

Main house

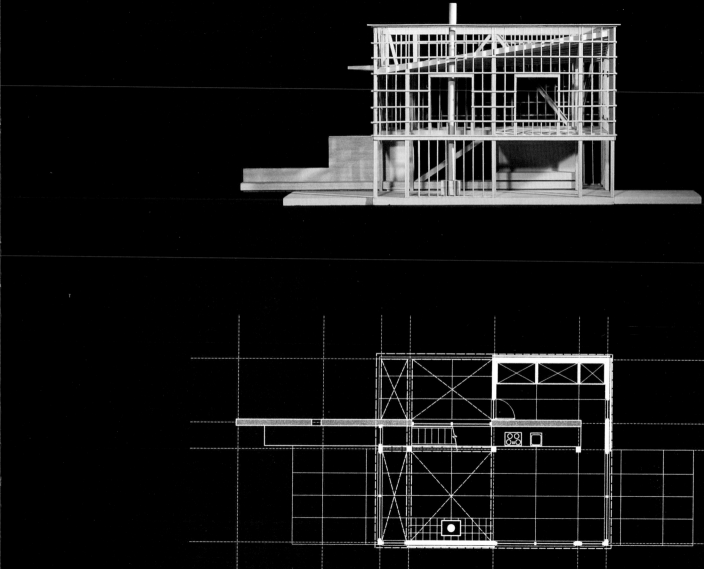

Urbanism

*There are two utopian traditions in architecture.
The first suggests that there is a need to start over
and build a new Jerusalem, while the second
accepts the world as it is and sees it as a place
to be improved.*

Whether located on a city street or a village road, the work of the practice begins as a response to context. It is connected to the process of settlement. Site plans are abstracted cognitive maps of the project which illustrate the building's role in the larger cultural landscape. Each building carries knowledge of the geomorphology of the site. As well as being a building design commission, each project is regarded as an environmental design study that is developed with an intent to improve the landscape and the city.

Consistent with an emphasis on modest means and the development of a grammar, it is the focus on the value of the urban fabric and the ordinary that helps to create memorable democratic places.

The following five projects include three urban infill projects and two university buildings located on city campuses. Two of the infill projects are 25'-0" apart and the third is a street away. They are clustered in Halifax's Peninsula North neighbourhood at the foot of the Citadel. Produced by development agreements, they represent a form of active resistance against the zoning that was proposed for an historic, working class neighbourhood – a zoning that would have likely resulted in the destruction of the remaining buildings. These projects collectively argue for a high-density, low-rise, mixed-use, zero-lot line form of development. They consolidate the urban fabric. The consequence was a change in the city zoning to permit this type of development in this part of Halifax.

Two projects involved the architect as developer, general contractor and user. Most were realised with shoestring budgets. Together they describe a life; a place for a family to live, a place to work and a school where architecture is taught. They are all located around the Citadel. Dolores Hayden has suggested that there are two utopian traditions in architecture. The first suggests that there is a need to start over and build a new Jerusalem, while the second accepts the world as it is and sees it as a place to be improved. This work seeks out the latter.

The thematic structure of this book is derived from three passions linked by a democratic ideal that is threaded through the complete body of work. It is intended to demystify one approach to design.

2042   2086   Maynard Street

Falkland Street

2098   Creighton Street

2042 & 2086 Maynard Street

Halifax, Nova Scotia, 1990 & 1993

2042 Maynard Street (above) and 2086 Maynard Street lot (top right) before the construction of new buildings

2042 MAYNARD STREET

Peninsula North, also known as the Old North End, is located at the foot of Halifax's Citadel Hill. It is the oldest suburb of the original colonial grid town and was developed in the early 1800s. This dense, working class neighbourhood seems appropriate for this live/work infill experiment. The project, which involved the architect as designer and developer, combines the reuse of a 1940s gas station to house an architect's office with the addition of four new infill town-houses. Three of these houses were designed to be sold. One was retained for the architect and his family. This affordable, mixed-use project was built at a cost of $65/ft.^2 on a small corner lot of 3,500 ft^2 by exploiting a development agreement process. It achieves a density that is higher than many of Halifax's high rise developments by providing ground-related units, parking and rooftop open space. The office and each of the townhouses have private individual access with separate street addresses.

The blue clapboard row houses continue the residential grain of Falkland Street and extend it into a block where the original houses had burned down. The gable-roofed rhombus containing the row houses refers to an arche-typal idea of 'street' and is built of light, timber frame construction. Given the structural plasticity of platform framing, holes are punched freely in the facade resulting in an informality which recalls vernacular building. The units are generic, side hall row houses built directly on the street line like their neighbours. Raised sit-com

entries allow the units to be sunken below the intersection between the wooden box houses and the concrete box of the office.

The concrete gas station containing the office is treated as a found object on Maynard Street. This open plan studio reverses the typical front-of-house/back-of-house organization of professional offices, by placing the administration at the back and the drawing studio at the front. There are no enclosed offices.

Highly finished totemic elements, including a black lacquer box which supports three 3" x 3'-0" x 12'-0" floating maple slabs that form desk tops, contrast with the raw concrete shell of the office building. A narrow stair, hidden in the black box, provides access to a meeting room placed within a rooftop shed. The result-ing roofscape with its red doghouse, yellow swing set, and turquoise shed resembles a rural Nova Scotia 'dog patch' landscape, brought into town, and protected by the wall of row houses.

2086 MAYNARD STREET

Three years after completing the project at 2042 Maynard Street, the opportunity arose to build a single family house on the opposite corner lot. This provided the possibility of con-tinuing the new piece of street frontage which had been constructed in 1990. This small lot, just 900 ft^2 in area, was the site of an earlier dwelling which had been destroyed by fire. A new house of 2,535 ft^2 with 110 percent site coverage was designed with the benefit of a development agreement. However these

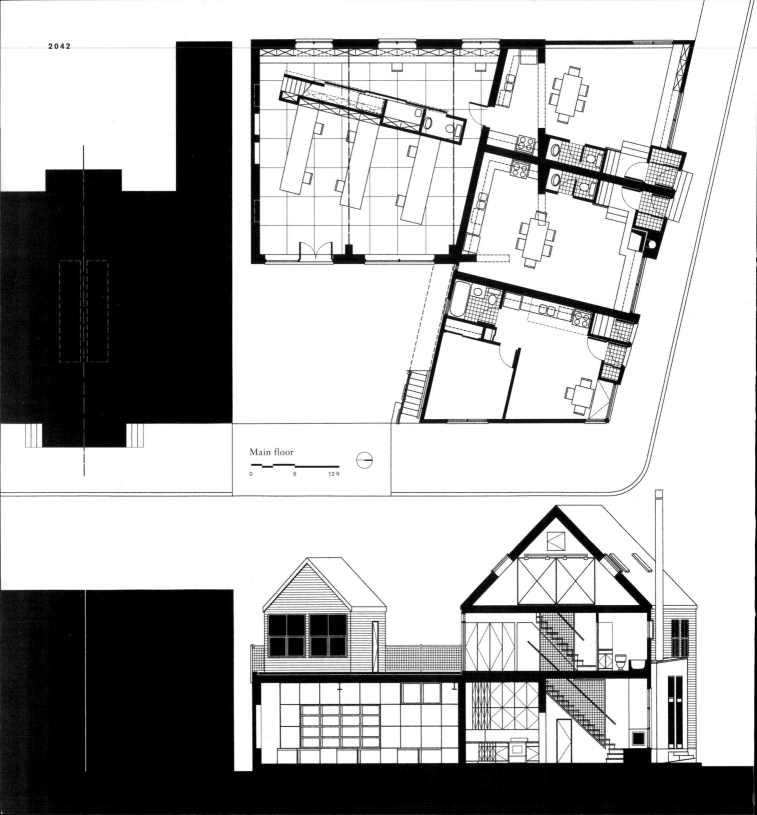

Main floor

0   6   12 ft

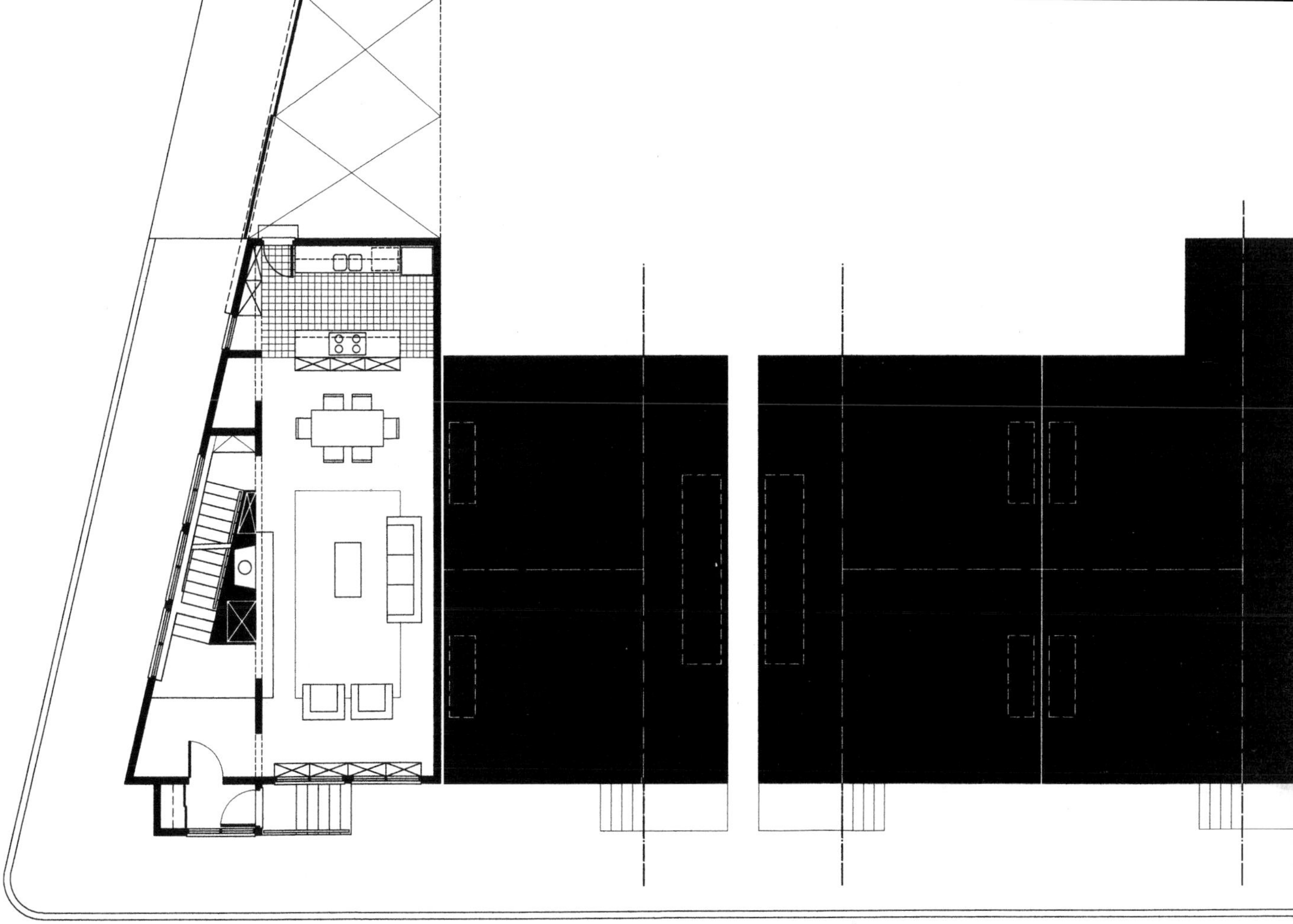

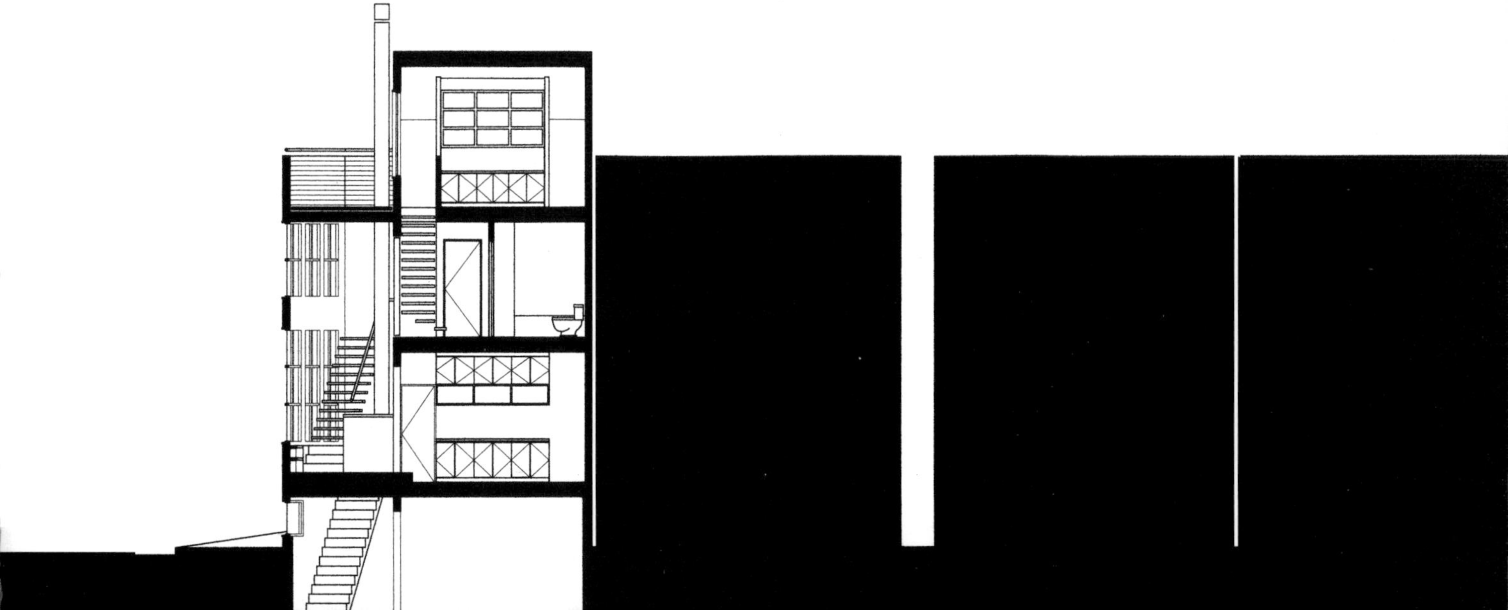

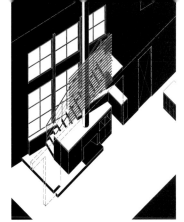

two projects, 25'-0 apart and designed over a three year period, follow somewhat different contextual design clues. This project is situated in a city block which is composed exclusively of two-storey row houses that are flat-topped boxes. The new building continues the street facade around the street corner.

This single family home provides a 40'-0 long great room, a basement, three bedrooms, two bathrooms, two parking spaces, two roof terraces and an 18'-0 tall hallway. It is a transformation of the grammar of the typical sidehall, flat-top box house which also maintains the two room deep form of the row house typical of this particular neighbourhood. A Halifax storm porch is built over the sidewalk and a traditional kitchen is extended into the rear yard. The front and rear parlours have been combined to create the open plan of the great room. The typical side hall is transformed into an 18'-0 tall, south-facing atrium between the entry and the great room. The parlour zone of the house is extruded through the section to be expressed as a modern rooftop penthouse which overlooks the harbour. The totemic elements are consolidated in the stair hall, creating a dense, sculptural, hearth-like element that gives focus to the house. This element, consisting of the fireplace, stair, a giant window and the lath wall forms a screen to provide privacy between home and street.

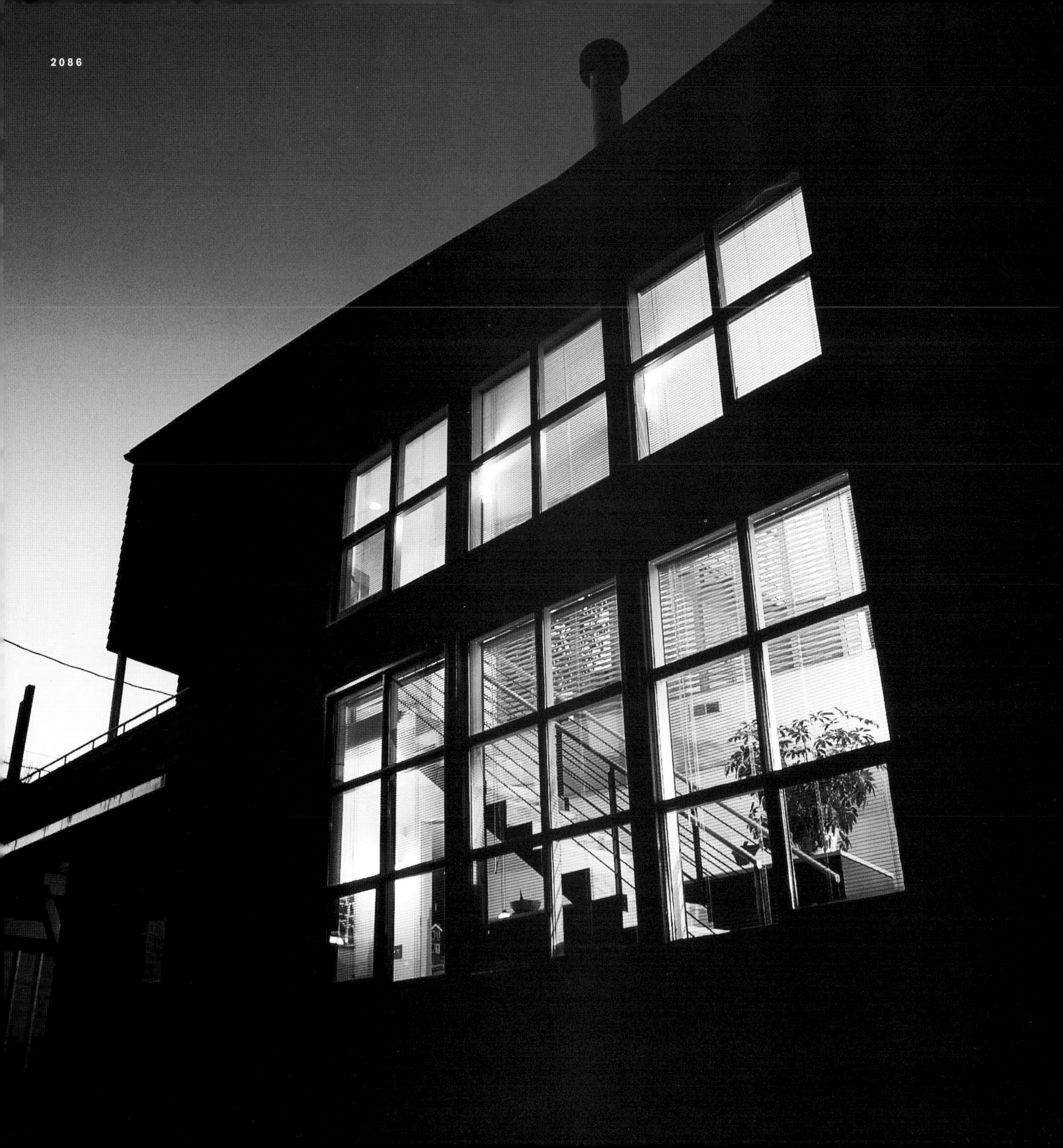

2098 Creighton Street

Halifax, Nova Scotia, 1988

In this experiment of urban infill in the Peninsula North neighbourhood of Halifax the architect was designer, developer and the user. The 3,000 ft^2 residential project provides three residential units and was built on an undersized lot of 2,000 ft^2 by development agreement. Historically Peninsula North has been a working class area of the city with a mix of residential, commercial and industrial uses. It is characterized by a high-density urban fabric which consists of small lots, flat, zero-lot-line streetscapes and simple building forms. This project was conceived as a prototype for affordable ($56/ft^2), high density, low rise, mid-block, infill housing. As a result, the design seeks to express generic or prototypical characteristics rather than exploring particular idiosyncratic qualities.

Two rental units of 750 ft^2 each occupy the basement and ground floor levels, while a larger unit planned for the owner occupies the two upper floors. All units have the feeling of townhouses. They separate living and sleeping levels and provide private street level entrances. Living areas are expressed as 40'-0 long 'shot gun' spaces, with floor-to-ceiling windows at both ends, and urbane 'blinders' consisting of service spaces running down both sides.

A tartan grid establishes both this spatial structure and the primary structural system for the building. The envelope is constructed of conventional platform framing, and clad in a zero-detailed clapboard skin reminiscent of the archetypal sheds that dot the rural landscape. The wood facade is revealed as a thin-skinned 'face' on the street, emphasizing cultural convention rather than the firewall required by the building code. Hot-dipped, galvanized steel entry steps and the hanging 'scallop-dragger' balcony are lightweight, folk-tech attachments to the facades.

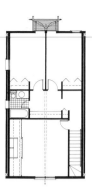

Third floor

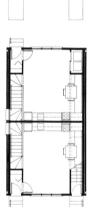

Second floor

Main floor

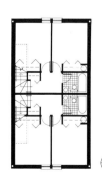

Basement

0   8   16 ft

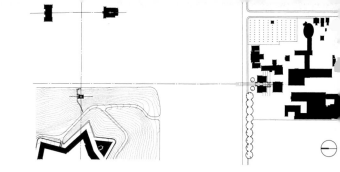

School of Architecture Addition

Halifax, Nova Scotia, 1993

This 'new room for architecture' at the Technical University of Nova Scotia was the winning scheme in an international design competition. It was a project with high aspirations and an extremely limited budget. If the competition process has the advantage of providing a rare opportunity for young architects, it also has the disadvantage of producing a design concept which has not benefited from a participatory design process.

The project is informed by studies of the built fabric of the city and the aspiration to provide a new room in the University which could be used by students, faculty and the community. Located on Spring Garden Road at the southern edge of the original colonial town grid, this new room is aligned with the Town Clock and is connected to George Street, which links the Citadel, City Hall and St. Pauls Church in the historic core of Halifax.

The project completes a formal procession of spaces from the Town Clock to the neo-classical porch of the existing school building and into the tall new room. A giant window in that room extends that sequence out with views across the harbour to the ocean beyond.

The project is a metal box inserted into the courtyard of the existing U-shaped school building and constructed over an existing auditorium. The addition completes the plan of the existing building. Glazed 'reveals' help to distinguish between the old and the new.

In the life of the architecture school this new room is conceived as infrastructure. It acts as a laboratory and an industrial work space where students can mock-up large installations, a place to exhibit work and a forum for public presentations.

As an educational space the project plays a didactic role. By exposing the components of the building's construction systems and revealing the hierarchy of their assembly the design attempts to make the process of construction legible. The design has been developed to allow for phased construction. The first phase, consisting of a freestanding braced steel frame toed under the mass of the existing brick building and clad in galvalume, was completed in 1993. Subsequent phases will create three additional infill studio floors.

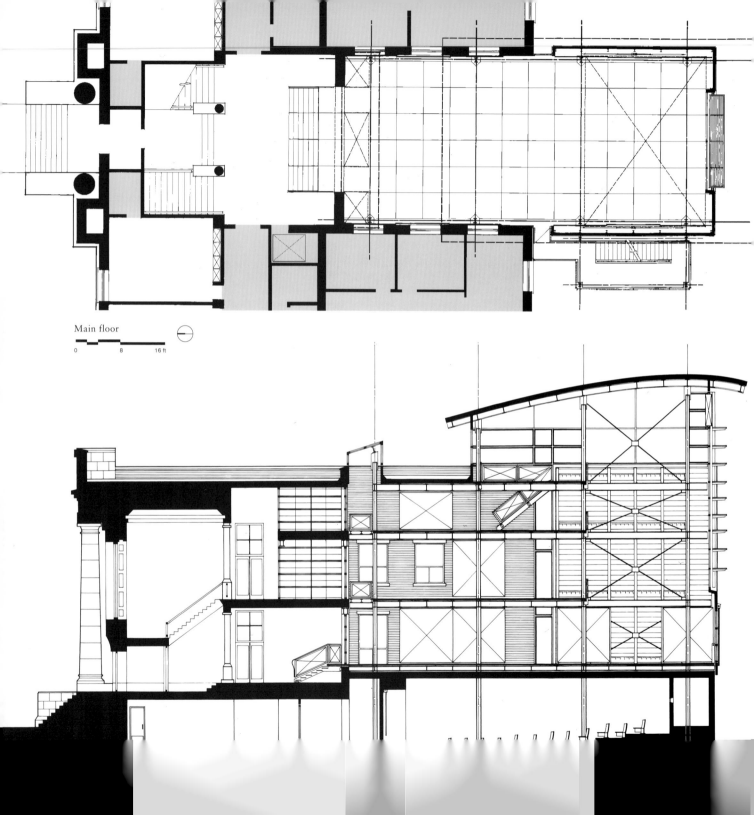

Main floor

0   8   16 ft

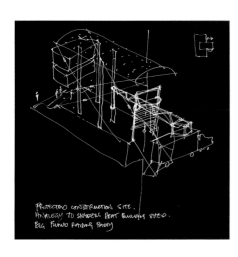

PROTECTED CONSTRUCTION SITE.
ANALOGY TO SNYDERS BOAT BUILDING SHED.
BIG FRAME RAISING PARTY

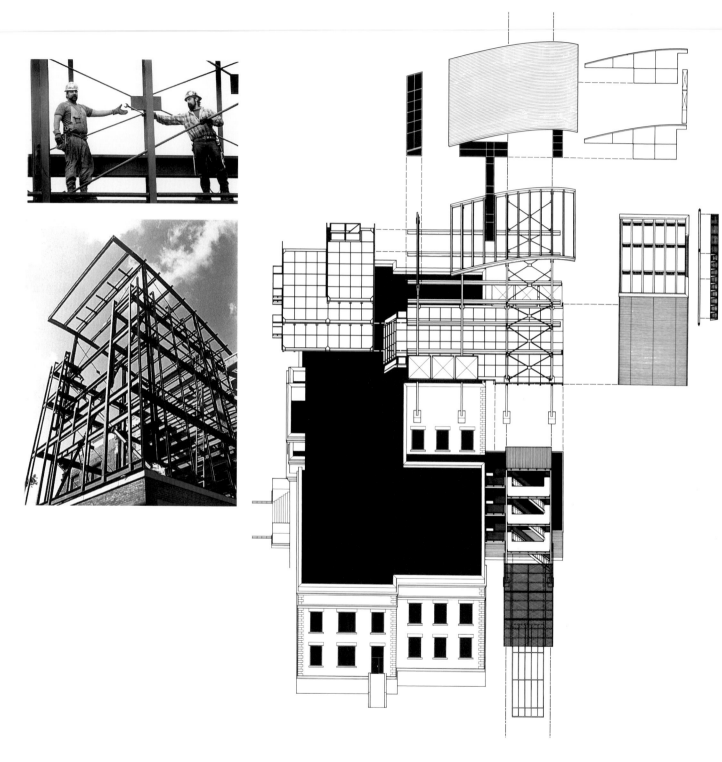

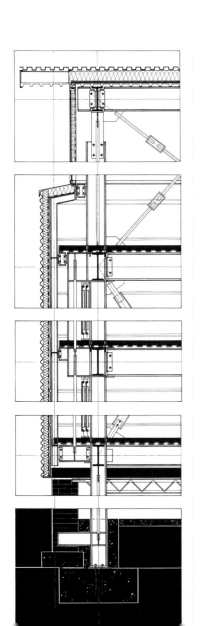

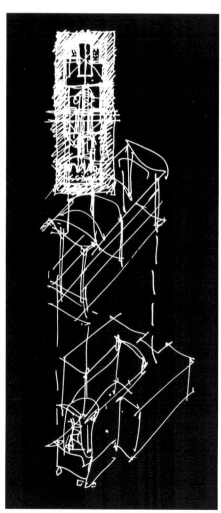

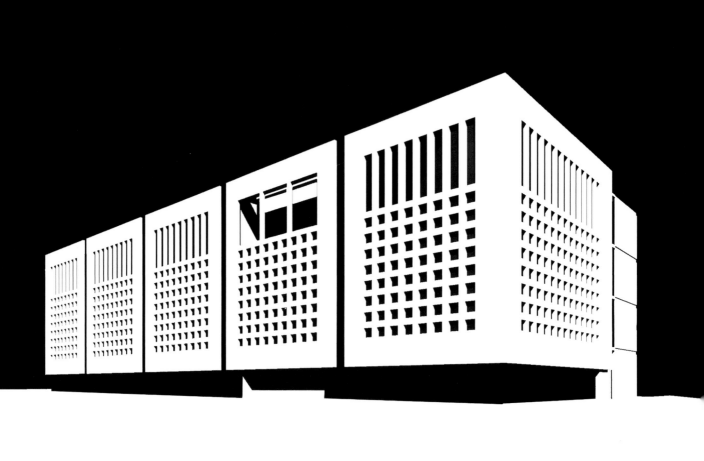

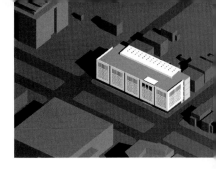

Faculty of Computer Science, Dalhousie University

Halifax, Nova Scotia, 1998

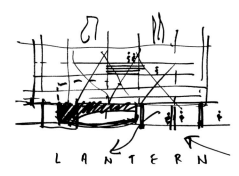

In 1991, Brian MacKay-Lyons led a team of architects and urban designers, including Charles Moore, Attilio Gobbi, William Mitchell and Giancarlo De Carlo to produce a Campus Plan for Dalhousie University. The result of a participatory design process involving the broader university community, the Campus Plan proposed that University Avenue be developed as a linear garden flanked by academic court-yard buildings. The new Computer Science Building is a product of both the Dalhousie Campus Plan and the recent merger of Dalhousie University and the Technical University of Nova Scotia. The project has been undertaken by Brian MacKay-Lyons Architecture Urban Design in association with Fowler, Bauld, and Mitchell Ltd., and William Mitchell as special consultant.

The program, developed in tandem with the scheme requires 85,000 ft^2 distributed in five storeys on a 200' x 100' site along University Avenue. The scheme embodies an academic philosophy which views computer science as an enabler in a multi-disciplinary research view of the University. Therefore, the heart of the program is the research 'playground' or electronic loft space aimed at project-based learning. A 65' tall 'cybercafe' is a social forum in the building aimed at the informal exchange of ideas. An electronic amphitheatre facilitates intellectual exchange within a larger community.

Connected to the goal of accessibility to other academic disciplines, industry, and the public, the building takes on a lantern-like character in order to suggest the work and technology inside. Playground / lab bays on two levels hover above a glazed classroom base with an industry-oriented penthouse above. The entrance from University Avenue, under folded zinc screens, connects to the atrium which will contain the cafe. The zinc screens are draped off a poured concrete structural frame, wrapping around the three street frontages and the atrium at the rear to form a minimalist urban metal jacket.

The project is scheduled to be completed in 1999.

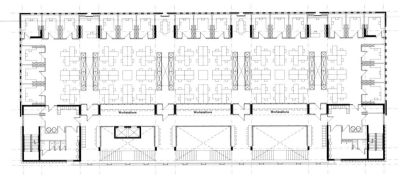

Levels Three and Four

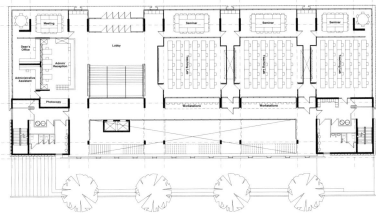

Level Two

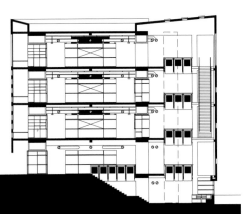

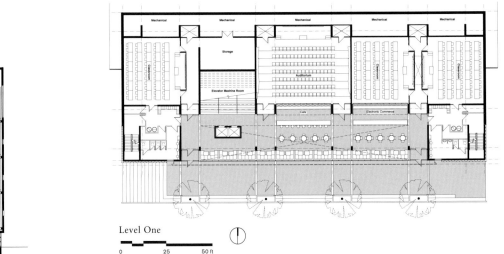

Level One

0   25   50 ft

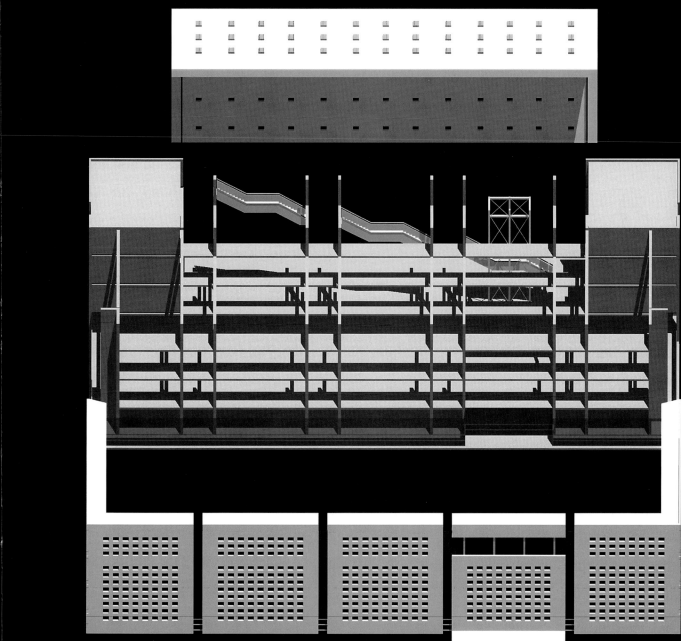

Postscript

Alex Colville

I have had a life-long interest in architecture and, over the years, two aspects of the work of Brian MacKay-Lyons have become particularly important to me.

Firstly, he is a native of Nova Scotia with both English and Acadian roots. Having first studied in this province and gone on to do post-graduate work at the University of California in Los Angeles, he chose to return to what can truly be described as his roots. It is the reversal of a trend which has made Nova Scotia poorer in every sense.

The second, is his interest in fundamental structure. Found in some local buildings of the past, it is structure which has a concomitant characteristic of being self-evident – not esoteric but exoteric – and not expensive. In this context I think of the house on Creighton Street. Built at low cost and as an adjunct to a street of old and modest houses, it directs attention to the serious need to design housing where people can live with dignity.

Appendices

Founded in 1985, the office of Brian MacKay-Lyons Architecture Urban Design is located in Halifax, Nova Scotia. The firm has developed a consistent body of work based on a modern regionalist architectural language which combines the use of archetypal forms with local building practices.

The work has gained both a local and international audience and has been widely published. The buildings which he has designed have received over 40 awards for design, including four Governor General's Awards – Canada's highest award for architectural excellence.

Brian MacKay-Lyons is a professor at Dalhousie University's Faculty of Architecture (formerly TUNS). He has lectured and taught internationally and in 1997 was Visiting Professor at Harvard Graduate School of Design.

Buildings and Projects

1980-1997

Dalhousie Faculty of Computer Science
Halifax, Nova Scotia, 1998-1999
Client: Dalhousie University
Architects: Brian MacKay-Lyons Architecture
Urban Design : Design Architects
Fowler, Bauld & Mitchell Ltd. : Architects and
Prime Consultant
Project Team: Brian MacKay-Lyons, Niall Savage,
Talbot Sweetapple, Tony Cook, George Coteras
Special Consultant: William Mitchell
Structural: D.J. Campbell Comeau Engineering
Mechanical/Electrical: Morris and Richards
Engineering
Acoustics: Atlantic Acoustic Consultants

La Ferme D'Acadie
Chebogue Point, Nova Scotia, 1998
Client: Chicory Farms
Architect: Brian MacKay-Lyons Architecture
Urban Design
Project Team: Brian MacKay-Lyons, Rob Meyer,
Darryl Jonas
Structural: D.J. Campbell Comeau Engineering

MacLauchlan House
West Covehead, Prince Edward Island, 1998
Client: Wade MacLauchlan
Architect: Brian MacKay-Lyons Architecture
Urban Design
Project Team: Brian MacKay-Lyons, Rob Meyer
Structural: D.J. Campbell Comeau Engineering

Kidd Beach House
Beach Meadows, Nova Scotia, 1998
Client: K.G. Kidd & Associates Ltd.
Architect: Brian MacKay-Lyons Architecture
Urban Design
Project Team: Brian MacKay-Lyons, Rob Meyer,
Susan Fitzgerald
Structural: D.J. Campbell Comeau Engineering
Builder: K.G.K. Construction

Attis House
Bois Joli, New Brunswick, 1998
Client: David and Margaret Attis
Architect: Brian MacKay-Lyons Architecture
Urban Design
Project Team: Brian MacKay-Lyons,
Talbot Sweetapple
Structural: D.J. Campbell Comeau Engineering

1997

Arts Education Community
Big Tancook Island, Nova Scotia, 1997-2002
Client: Gary Knowles, Ardra Cole
Architect: Brian MacKay-Lyons Architecture
Urban Design
Project Team: Brian MacKay-Lyons, Rob Meyer,
Susan Fitzgerald, Darryl Jonas
Structural: D.J. Campbell Comeau Engineering

Fulcher / Sapos House
Oxner's Head, Nova Scotia, 1997-1998
Client: Mary Ann Sapos and Wayne Fulcher
Architect: Brian MacKay-Lyons Architecture
Urban Design
Project Team: Brian MacKay-Lyons, Rob Meyer,
Bruno Weber, Marc Cormier
Structural: D.J. Campbell Comeau Engineering
Landscape: EDM Environmental Design and
Management Ltd.
Builder: Everts-Lind Enterprises (Richard Lind)

Le Village Historique Acadien De La Nouvelle Ecosse
Pubnico Ouest, Nouvelle Ecosse, 1997-1998
Client: Le Village Historique Acadien De La
Nouvelle Ecosse
Architect: Brian MacKay-Lyons Architecture
Urban Design
Project Team: Brian MacKay-Lyons, Marc Cormier,
Darryl Jonas
Structural: D.J. Campbell Comeau Engineering
Landscape: EDM Environmental Design and
Management Ltd.
Material Culture: Bernard LeBlanc

Kutcher House
Herring Cove, Nova Scotia, 1997-1998
Client: Jan and Stan Kutcher
Architect: Brian MacKay-Lyons Architecture
Urban Design
Project Team: Brian MacKay-Lyons, Rob Meyer,
Trevor Davies
Structural: D.J. Campbell Comeau Engineering
Builder: Special Projects (Faisal Forhart)

Maud Lewis Memorial

Marshalltown, Nova Scotia, 1997

Client: Art Gallery of Nova Scotia and
Maud Lewis Painted House Society

Architect: Brian MacKay-Lyons Architecture
Urban Design

Project Team: Brian MacKay-Lyons, Trevor
Davies, Darryl Jonas, Tony Gillis

Structural: D.J. Campbell Comeau Engineering

Fabrication: Cherubini Metal Workers

Ghost 1997

Upper Kingsburg, Nova Scotia, 1997

Architect/Professor: Brian MacKay-Lyons

Design/Build Team: Brian MacKay-Lyons
with Mehira Ebdel Aziz, Ben Duffell, Mike
Farrar, Nicola Grigg, Ron Isaac, Viktoria
Mygoro, Richard Nowlan, Trevor Thimm,
Krista Wuerr

Tribute: Beulah Oxner (Village Elder)

1996

Conde House

Lower Kingsburg, Nova Scotia, 1996-1998

Client: Carolyn and Michael Conde

Architect: Brian MacKay-Lyons Architecture
Urban Design

Project Team: Brian MacKay-Lyons,
Susan Fitzgerald

Structural: D.J. Campbell Comeau Engineering

Builder: Can-Do Industries (Robert Schmeisser)

Agnew House

First South Cove, Nova Scotia, 1996-1998

Client: Carley and Barry Agnew

Architect: Brian MacKay-Lyons Architecture
Urban Design

Project Team: Brian MacKay-Lyons, Darryl Jonas,
Fabien Pessant, Talbot Sweetapple

Structural: D.J. Campbell Comeau Engineering

Danielson House

Smelt Brook, Nova Scotia, 1996-1998

Client: Esther and Bill Danielson

Architect: Brian MacKay-Lyons Architecture
Urban Design

Project Team: Brian MacKay-Lyons, Bruno Weber,
Trevor Davies, Darryl Jonas

Structural: D.J. Campbell Comeau Engineering

Builder: Andrew Watts

Messenger House

Jollimore, Nova Scotia, 1996-1997

Client: Mary and John Messenger

Architect: Brian MacKay-Lyons Architecture
Urban Design

Project Team: Brian MacKay-Lyons, Darryl Jonas,
Doug Wigle, Tony Gillis

Structural: D.J. Campbell Comeau Engineering

Builder: Special Projects Ltd. (Faisal Forhart)

Steadman / Roth House

Cambrian Cove, Nova Scotia, 1996-1997

Client: Cheryl Steadman and Jason Roth

Architect: Brian MacKay-Lyons Architecture
Urban Design

Project Team: Brian MacKay-Lyons, Darryl
Jonas, Trevor Davies, Bruno Weber

Structural: D.J. Campbell Comeau Engineering

Builder: Andrew Watts

The LaHave House Project

Automated Architectural Design, 1996

Research Principals: Brian MacKay-Lyons,
Dr. Andrew Rau-Chaplin

Project Team: Brian MacKay-Lyons, Dr. Andrew
Rau-Chaplin, Peter-Frank Spierenburg, Trevor
Davies, Peter Greg, Robert Gregory Power,
Guiyan Cao, Emanuel Jannasch, Jason Smirnis,
Marco Bonaventura, Weihua He, Chad Seward,
Timmy Doucette, Jedrzej Gajewski, Xiangqun Hu

1995

Howard House

West Pennant, Nova Scotia, 1995-1998

Client: Vivian and David Howard

Architect: Brian MacKay-Lyons Architecture
Urban Design

Project Team: Brian MacKay-Lyons, Niall
Savage, Talbot Sweetapple, Trevor Davies

Structural: D.J. Campbell Comeau Engineering

Builder: Andrew Watts

House on the Nova Scotia Coast #12

South Shore of Nova Scotia, 1995-1997
Architect: Brian MacKay-Lyons Architecture
Urban Design
Project Team: Brian MacKay-Lyons, Niall Savage,
Doug Wigle, Bruno Weber, Tony Gillis,
HilaryBackman
Structural: D.J. Campbell Comeau Engineering
Landscape: EDM Environmental Design and
Management Ltd.
Builder: Cyril Smith

Banque Royale

Pubnico Ouest, Nouvelle Ecosse, 1995-1996
Client: The Royal Bank of Canada
- Real Estate Operations: John Rowe
- Bank Manager: Gerry Hubbard
Architect: Brian MacKay-Lyons Architecture
Urban Design
Project Team: Brian MacKay-Lyons, Doug Wigle,
Niall Savage, Tony Gillis
Structural: D.J. Campbell Comeau Engineering
Mechanical: G.S. Ewert Engineering
Electrical: Strum Engineering
Builder: Delmar Construction (Mark Bourque)

2 x 4 '95

Upper Kingsburg, Nova Scotia, 1995
Architect/Professor: Brian MacKay-Lyons
Design/Build Team: Brian MacKay-Lyons
with Chris Allen, Audrey Archambault,
Trevor Davies, Stephanie Forsythe,
RodGillis, Alistair Huber, Philip Jefferson,
David Jensen, Colleen Lashuk,
Alison MacNeil, John MacNeil, Chris Oxner,
Michael Rudnicki, Jason Smirnis
Structural: Michel Comeau

1994

Gaines House

Barrios Head, Nova Scotia, 1994-1998
Client: Patricia and Charles Gaines
Architect: Brian MacKay-Lyons Architecture
Urban Design
Project Team: Brian MacKay-Lyons, Darryl Jonas,
Rob Meyer, Talbot Sweetapple, Niall Savage,
Susan Fitzgerald, Marc Cormier
Structural: D.J. Campbell Comeau Engineering
Landscape: EDM Environmental Design and
Management Ltd.

Currie/McCall House

Halls Harbour, Nova Scotia, 1994-1996
Client: Jo Currie and Michael McCall
Architect: Brian MacKay-Lyons Architecture
Urban Design
Project Team: Brian MacKay-Lyons, Niall Savage,
John Dewolfe, Tony Gillis
Structural: D.J. Campbell Comeau Engineering
Builder: Andrew Watts

White/Leger House

Bayfield, Nova Scotia, 1994
Client: Helen Leger and Wendell White
Architect: Brian MacKay-Lyons Architecture
Urban Design
Project Team: Brian MacKay-Lyons, Niall Savage,
John Geldart
Structural: Archie Frost
Builder: Wendell White

Leahey House

Pugwash, Nova Scotia, 1994
Client: Dennice and Stephen Leahey
Architect: Brian MacKay-Lyons Architecture
Urban Design
Project Team: Brian MacKay-Lyons, Niall Savage,
John Geldart
Structural: D.J. Campbell Comeau Engineering
Landscape: Reinhart Petersmann - EDM Environmental
Design and Management Ltd.
Builder: Arthur Baxter

Ghost '94

Upper Kingsburg, Nova Scotia, 1994

Architect/Professor: Brian MacKay-Lyons

Design/Build Team: Brian MacKay-Lyons

with Matthew Beattie, Nicole Delmage,

Caralyn Jeffs, Glen MacMullin, Zane Murdoch,

Jim Pfeffer, Sean Rodrigues, Talbot Sweetapple,

Michael Woodland

1993

2086 Maynard Street

Halifax, Nova Scotia, 1993

Client: Maureen and Chris Millier

Architect: Brian MacKay-Lyons Architecture

Urban Design

Project Team: Brian MacKay-Lyons, Niall Savage,

John Geldart

Structural: Archie Frost

Builder: Gordon MacLean

Confederation Birthplace Competition

Charlottetown, Prince Edward Island, 1993

Clients: CADC (Charlottetown Area Development

Corporation)

Architects: Brian MacKay-Lyons Architecture

Urban Design

Project Team: Brian MacKay-Lyons,

Charles Fawkes, Jeff Kirby, Lois Luke

Landscape: Reinhart Petersmann, EDM

Environmental Design and Management Ltd.

Civil: Harland Associates

1992

LeGallais House

Bedford, Nova Scotia, 1992

Client: Susan and Brad LeGallais

Architect: Brian MacKay-Lyons Architecture

Urban Design

Project Team: Brian MacKay-Lyons, Andrew King,

Brenda Webster, Niall Savage

Structural: D.J. Campbell Comeau Engineering

Builder: Gordon MacLean

1991

School of Architecture Extension

Technical University of Nova Scotia

Halifax, Nova Scotia, 1991-1993

Client: The Technical University of Nova Scotia

Architect: Brian MacKay-Lyons Architecture

Urban Design

Project Team: Brian MacKay-Lyons, Attilio Gobbi,

Bob Benz, Michael Carroll, Tony Gillis,

John Geldart, Niall Savage, Andrew King,

Brenda Webster

Structural: D.J. Campbell Comeau Engineering

Mechanical: G.S. Ewert Engineering

Electrical: Strum Engineering

Builder: Dineen Construction

Yaukey Cottage

Blanche Peninsula, Nova Scotia, 1991

Client: Barbara and David Yaukey

Architect: Brian MacKay-Lyons Architecture

Urban Design

Project Team: Brian MacKay-Lyons, Bob Benz,

Michael Carroll, Niall Savage

Structural: Tom Harland

Builder: Gordon MacLean

Dalhousie Campus Plan

Halifax, Nova Scotia, 1991

Client: Dalhousie University

Architect: Brian MacKay-Lyons Architecture

Urban Design

Consultants: Charles W. Moore, Attilio Gobbi,

William Mitchell, Giancarlo De Carlo

Project Team: Brian MacKay-Lyons, Attilio Gobbi,

Charles Moore, William Mitchell, Michael Carroll,

Andrew King, Giancarlo De Carlo, John Geldart

1990

Peacekeeping Monument Competition
Ottawa, Ontario, 1990
Client: National Capital Commission, Department
of National Defence
Architect: Brian MacKay-Lyons Architecture
Urban Design
Artist: Michael Snow
Project Team: Brian MacKay-Lyons,
Michael Snow, Bob Benz, Michael Carroll
Structural: Tom Harland

1989

Gibson/Livingston House
Site - Confidential, 1989-1990
Client: Peter Livingston, Patti Livingston,
Gary Gibson, Laura Gibson
Architect: Brian MacKay-Lyons Architecture
Urban Design
Project Team: Brian MacKay-Lyons, Bob Benz,
Michael Carroll, Joachim Hardt, Gary Fields
Structural: D.J. Campbell Comeau Engineering
Landscape: Reinhart Petersmann
Builder: Everts-Lind Enterprises (Richard Lind),
Gordon MacLean

2042 Maynard Street
Halifax, Nova Scotia, 1989-1990
Client: Marilyn and Brian MacKay-Lyons
Architect: Brian MacKay-Lyons Architecture
Urban Design
Project Team: Brian MacKay-Lyons,
Michael Carroll, Andrew King, Bob Benz,
Gary Fields,
Joachim Hardt
Structural: Archie Frost
Builder: Gordon MacLean

Lea House
Indian Point, Nova Scotia, 1989
Client: Anne and Bob Lea
Architect: Brian MacKay-Lyons Architecture
Urban Design
Project Team: Brian MacKay-Lyons,
Michael Carroll, Joachim Hardt
Structural: D.J. Campbell Comeau Engineering
Landscape: Reinhart Petersmann
Builder: Cyril Smith

Rubadoux/Cameron Studio
Rose Bay, Nova Scotia, 1989
Client: Craig Rubadoux and Mary Cameron
Architect: Brian MacKay-Lyons Architecture
Urban Design
Project Team: Brian MacKay-Lyons, Gary Fields,
Andrew King, Niall Savage
Structural: D.J. Campbell Comeau Engineering
Builder: Everts-Lind Enterprises (Richard Lind)

Wicht/MacNeill Cottage
Lower Kingsburg, Nova Scotia, 1989
Client: Arnold Wicht, Deborah MacNeill
Architect: Brian MacKay-Lyons Architecture
Urban Design
Project Team: Brian MacKay-Lyons,
Gary Fields, Andrew King
Structural: D.J. Campbell Comeau Engineering
Builder: Can-Do Industries (Robert Schmeisser)

5288 South Street Infill
Halifax, Nova Scotia, 1989
Clients: Wade MacLachlan, Alan Fine
Architect: Brian MacKay-Lyons Architecture
Urban Design
Project Team: Brian MacKay-Lyons, Niall Savage,
Bob Benz
Structural: D.J. Campbell Comeau Engineering
Builder: Arconstruct (Bob Benz)

1988

2098 Creighton Street
Halifax, Nova Scotia, 1988
Client: Marilyn and Brian MacKay-Lyons
Architect: Brian MacKay-Lyons Architecture
Urban Design
Project Team: Brian MacKay-Lyons, Bob Benz
Structural: Archie Frost
Builder: Arconstruct (Bob Benz)

Nielsen/White House

Halifax, Nova Scotia, 1988

Client: Christine Nielsen, George White

Architect: Brian MacKay-Lyons Architecture
Urban Design

Project Team: Brian MacKay-Lyons,
Patrick MacLachlan, Michael Carroll, Bob Benz,
Brent Ash, Andrew King, Michael Bryant,
Stephen Conger

Structural: M.S. Yolles & Partners (Roland
Bergman)

Olympic Arches Competition

Calgary, Alberta, 1988

Client: Olympic Arts Festival

Architect: Brian MacKay-Lyons Architecture
Urban Design

Project Team: Brian MacKay-Lyons, Bob Benz,
Michael Carroll

Canadian Clay and Glass Gallery Competition

Waterloo, Ontario, 1987

Architects: Design Architects - Brian MacKay-
Lyons Architecture Urban Design

Associate Architects: Duffus, Romans, Kundzins,
and Rounsefell

Design Team: Brian MacKay-Lyons, Attilio Gobbi,
Bob Benz, Brenda Webster

Structural: Tom Harland

2020 Maynard Street

(Public Housing Infill)

Halifax, Nova Scotia, 1986

Client: Halifax Non-Profit Housing Society

Architect: Brian MacKay-Lyons Architecture
Urban Design

Project Team: Brian MacKay-Lyons, Bob Benz

Structural: Archie Frost

Builder: Ecos Construction

House on the Nova Scotia Coast #1

Upper Kingsburg, Nova Scotia, 1985-1986

Client: Marilyn and Brian MacKay-Lyons

Architect: Brian MacKay-Lyons Architecture
Urban Design

Project Team: Brian MacKay-Lyons, Bob Benz,
Therese LeBlanc, Tom Emodi

Structural: D.J. Campbell Comeau Engineering

Builder: Can-Do Industries (Robert Schmeisser)

Carr House

Parkdale, Prince Edward Island, 1985

Client: Connie and John Carr

Architect: Emodi, MacKay-Lyons, Architects

Project Team: Brian MacKay-Lyons, Bob Benz,
Tom Emodi, Therese LeBlanc

Structural: D.J. Campbell Comeau

Builder: Charles MacDonald

2476 Robie Street Condominiums

(First Baptist Church Renovations)

Halifax, Nova Scotia, 1985

Client: Phillip Levangie

Architect: Emodi, MacKay-Lyons, Architects

Project Team: Brian MacKay-Lyons, Bob Benz,
Therese LeBlanc, Tom Emodi, Chris Von Maltzahn

Lyons Tower

Five Island Lake, Nova Scotia, 1979-1980

Client: Renee and David Lyons

Architect: Networks Limited

Project Team: Brian MacKay-Lyons,
Larry Richards, Eric Fiss

Builder: Ninos Construction (George Ninos)

Awards

1998

The Lieutenant Governor's Award of Merit

Banque Royale, Pubnico Ouest, Nouvelle Ecosse

1997

The Governor General's Medal for Architecture

House on the Nova Scotia Coast #12

The Lieutenant Governor's Citation

House on the Nova Scotia Coast #12

1996

The Canadian Architect Award of Excellence

Howard House, West Pennant, Nova Scotia

The Lieutenant Governor's Citation

White/Leger House, Antigonish, Nova Scotia

1995

The Lieutenant Governor's Medal of Excellence

Leahey House, Pugwash, Nova Scotia

1994

The Governor General's Award for Architecture

Leahey House, Pugwash, Nova Scotia

The Lieutenant Governor's Award of Merit

2086 Maynard Street, Halifax, Nova Scotia

1993

The Canadian Architect Award of Excellence

Leahey House, Pugwash, Nova Scotia

The Lieutenant Governor's Medal of Excellence

LeGallais House, Bedford, Nova Scotia

1992

The Governor General's Medal for Architecture

2042 Maynard Street, Mixed Use Infill,
Halifax, Nova Scotia

The Lieutenant Governor's Award of Merit

Yaukey Cottage, Blanche Peninsula, Nova Scotia

The Lieutenant Governor's Awards

Honourable Mention, Dalhousie Campus Plan
"A Collective Vision", Halifax, Nova Scotia

1991

The Lieutenant Governor's Medal of Excellence

2042 Maynard Street, Mixed Used Infill,
Halifax, Nova Scotia

The Lieutenant Governor's Award

Honourable Mention, Lea House,
St. Margaret's Bay, Nova Scotia

1990

First Prize, International Design Competition

A 'New Room' for Architecture: design
for an Extension to The School of Architecture,
Technical University of Nova Scotia,
Halifax, Nova Scotia

The Lieutenant Governor's Medal of Excellence

Gibson/Livingston House,
Sherbrooke Lake, Nova Scotia

The Lieutenant Governor's Award of Merit

Wicht Cottage, Lower Kingsburg, Nova Scotia

1989

Nova Scotia Association of Architects Award of Merit

2098 Creighton Street, Infill Housing,
Halifax, Nova Scotia

Nova Scotia Association of Architects Citation

Nielsen/White House, Halifax, Nova Scotia

1988

The Canadian Architect Award of Excellence

Nielsen/White House, Halifax, Nova Scotia

The Olympic Arts Medal

Gate for Olympic Games, Olympic Arts Festival,
Calgary, Alberta

The Royal Society of the Arts

Honourable Mention

Medal of Excellence

Nova Scotia Association of Architects,
Peninsula North Infill Housing Strategy
2020 Maynard Street, Halifax, Nova Scotia.

Prix De Rome: Finalist

The First Canadian Prix De Rome

Nova Scotia Association of Architects Citation

Canadian Clay and Glass Gallery Competition,
Waterloo, Ontario.

The Governor General's Medal for Architecture

House on the Nova Scotia Coast, Renovation,
Upper Kingsburg, Nova Scotia.

Award of Excellence

Nova Scotia Association of Architects,
First Baptist Church, Renovation to Housing,
(Emodi/MacKay- Lyons),
Halifax, Nova Scotia

Heritage Canada Restoration Award

Windermere House, Restoration/Renovation,
Charlottetown, Prince Edward Island

Nova Scotia Association of Architects Citation

House on the Nova Scotia Coast, Renovation,
Upper Kingsburg, Nova Scotia.

Halifax Non-Profit Housing Society Competition

First Prize, Infill Housing, Halifax, Nova Scotia

Bibliography

1998

Ten Houses: Brian MacKay-Lyons
Monograph to be published by Rockport Publishers, Rockport, Massachusetts.

International Architecture Yearbook
Features House on the NS Coast #12, Images Australia, Victoria, Australia, April, pp. 306-09.

Architecture in Wood
Features LeGallais House, Lawrence King Publishing, London, UK.

Detail, 2/98
Stairs Issue; Features Messenger House, Munich Germany, March / April, pp. 164-66.

Detail, 1/98
Features Ghost #3, Modest Building Design Issue, Munich, Germany, January / February, pp. 22-23

1997

Canadian Architect
1997 Awards Issue; Brian MacKay-Lyons - Juror, "Shades of Green". Southam Publications: Don Mills, Ontario. Vol. 42, No. 12, pp. 15-37.

Le Devoir
Un Phare Dans La Tempête – Profile on Brian MacKay-Lyons Architecture + Urban Design, by Sophie Gironnay, November 30, p. D12.

Union Internationale Des Architects
Award Winning Architecture – International Yearbook 1997; Features: House on the Nova Scotia Coast #12; Munich, Germany; Editor: Frantisek Sedlacek, p. 184.

The Montreal Gazette
"Brian MacKay-Lyons' Award-winning Coast Houses", by Rhys Phillips, July 4, pp. 1 & 5.

Architecture Canada 1997
The Governor General's Awards for Architecture, Features: House on the Nova Scotia Coast #12, Royal Architectural Institute of Canada, Tuns Press; June, ISBN 0-929112-38-5, pp. 40-47.

Globe and Mail
Profile on the career of Brian MacKay-Lyons, by Rhys Phillips, April 12.

International Architecture Yearbook
House on the Nova Scotia Coast #9, Images Australia, Vol. III, Mulgrave, Victoria, Australia, April, pp. 296-97.

The Canadian Architect
Features: House on the Nova Scotia Coast #12; Vol. 42, No. 2, pp. 24-25.

1996

The Canadian Architect
1996 Canadian Architect Awards of Excellence; Features: The Howard House; Vol. 41, No. 12, pp. 44-46.

The Canadian Architect
Yolles on Structure; Features: House on the Nova Scotia Coast #9 , & House on the Nova Scotia Coast #12; Vol. 41, No. 11, p. 31.

Dictionnaire D'Architecture Contemporaine
Leahey House included in this encyclopedia of 20th century world architecture. Critic: Andrew Gruft; Paris, France.

Studio Works 4
Features work of Brian MacKay-Lyons' Options Studio, Harvard Graduate School of Design; Spring, pp. 112-113.

1995

Design Quarterly 165
"Seven Stories from a Village Architect", Brian MacKay-Lyons, (Monograph featuring 16 projects); Editor: Robert A. Jensen; Minneapolis, M.I.T. Press, Cambridge, Massachusetts, Summer.

At Home in Canada
Features: 2042 Maynard Street and House on the Nova Scotia Coast #1, along with 22 other Canadian homes and families; Book by Hilary Weston and Nicole Eaton; Viking Press, pp. 62-69.

Progressive Architecture

Features: Profile of firm, titled "Folk-Tech", documenting 10 years of projects (Howard House, 2042 Maynard Street, LeGallais House, Leahey House, Yaukey Cottage, White/Leger House, 'Ghost' Pavilion, TUNS Architecture Addition). Article by Thomas Fisher, Editorial Director; Stanford, Connecticut; August, pp. 62-72.

The Canadian Architect

Article titled 'A Life on the Wing', remembering the late Jon Murray; Vol. 40, No. 7, p. 34.

Canada 43¢ Stamp

Commemorating the 100th anniversary of Lunenburg Academy, designed by Brian MacKay-Lyons with Stephen Slipp; launched June 1995, 18 million printed.

1994

Interpretations of Nature

Canadian Architecture, Landscape Architecture and Urbanism, Catalogue; Features: Leahey House; Editor: George Kapelos; p. 42.

1994 Governor General's Awards

Features: House on the Nova Scotia Coast #9; Royal Architectural Institute of Canada; Editor: Graham Owen; pp. 190-197.

The Canadian Architect

Education Buildings Issue: A Room in a School; Features: TUNS Architecture Addition Phase 1; by Brian Carter; May.

The Ottawa Citizen

'Tradition and Abstraction' - Profile featuring: LeGallais House, Kingsburg House, Gibson-Livingston House; by Rhys Phillips; April 9, Sec. 1, p. 1.

The Canadian Architect

Houses in the City; Features: 2086 Maynard Street. by Paul Symes; April, Vol. 39, No. 4, pp. 20-21.

The Canadian Architect

Article: In Memoriam to Charles Moore; February, Vol. 39, No. 2, p. 5.

1993

The Canadian Architect

1993 Awards of Excellence - Leahey House; December, Vol. 38, No. 12, pp. 16-17.

Canadian House and Home,

The Surprising Barns of Brian MacKay-Lyons. A profile of the firm featuring: Lea House, Wicht Cottage, Kingsburg House, Gibson-Livingston House, 2042 Maynard Street and LeGallais House. By Larry Richards, October, Vol. 15, No. 6, pp. 74-80.

The Architectural Review

Canada's New Wave. Features: Gibson-Livingston House and Yaukey Cottage. By Mary Miles; London, U.K.; May, Vol. 193, No. 1155, pp. 62-66.

1992

The Canadian Architect

Features: 2042 Maynard Street, the 1992 Governor General's Awards, November, Vol. 37, No. 11, pp. 22-25.

1992 Governor General's Awards

Features: 2042 Maynard Street – Mixed Use Infill; pp. 46-51

The Canadian Clay & Glass Gallery

Book published by Tuns Press, 1992, pp. 55-61

The Canadian Architect

A Collective Vision for Dalhousie; by Douglas MacLeod; May, Vol. 37, No. 5, pp. 25-29.

1991

A Collective Vision

A Campus Plan for Dalhousie; by Brian MacKay-Lyons with Charles Moore, William Mitchell, Attilo Gobbi, and Giancarlo De Carlo; July.

Peacekeeping Monument Competition Catalogue

Collaboration with Michael Snow. Published by The National Capital Commission.

Detail

Modest Building; Features: Rubadoux Studio (cover); by Claudia Capeller; Munich; April-May, pp.126-28.

1990

A New Room for Architecture

The Record of an Architectural Competition; TUNS Press, Halifax, Nova Scotia, 1990, pp.18-21.

The Architectural Review

Regional Perspectives, Maritime Journey. Features: 2042 Maynard Street, 2098 Creighton Steet, Rubadoux Studio, Gibson-Livingston, Wicht Cottage, Kingsburg; by Brian Carter; London, U.K.; November, Vol. 187, No. 1125, pp. 68-76.

The Canadian Architect

Eight Young Firms; September, Vol. 35, No. 9, pp. 34-35.

The Canadian Architect

Between 'Convention and Invention'; Features: 5288 South Street and 2098 Creighton Street (cover); June, Vol. 35, No. 6, pp. 17-21.

1988

Canadian Art

The Favourite Game; Features: Olympic Arch. By Ellen Tofflemire; Winter, Vol. 5, No. 4, pp. 76-83.

The Canadian Architect

1988 Awards of Excellence; Features: Nielsen/White House; December, Vol. 33, No. 12, pp. 34-36.

Chatelaine

Putting the Wow in Canadian Design. By Trudy Nelson; March, Vol. 61, No. 3, pp. 124-131.

1987

House Beautiful

Uplifting Addition, House on the Nova Scotia Coast. By Susan Zevon; New York; June, Vol. 129, No. 6, pp. 92-95.

Arts Atlantic

Brian MacKay-Lyons: Seeking Metaphors in Atlantic Architecture, Firm Profile; Features: Carr House, Kingsburg, Lyons Tower. By Laura Brandon; Summer/Fall, Vol. 8, No. 1, pp. 33-36.

Center

Centre for the Study of American Architecture, New Regionalist, Four Approaches to Regionalism in Recent Canadian Architecture. By Trevor Boddy; Austin, Texas; February, Vol. 3, p. 105.

1986

The Canadian Architect

Focus on Atlantic Canada. November. "A Sense of Place", by Brian MacKay-Lyons, pp. 20-21; "Invention and Reflection, House on the Nova Scotia Coast", by David Sisam, pp. 32-37, Vol. 31, No. 11.

Architecture

Journal of the American Institute of Architects, Annual Review of Recent World Architecture, Canada: A Sampling of the Nation's Far-Flung Works of Quality. By Odie Henault; Washington, D.C.; Septemberr, Vol. 75, No. 9, pp. 68-71.

The 1986 Governor General's Awards

House on the Nova Scotia Coast; pp. 111-14

1982

O KANADA

Architecture in Canada since 1950, Lyons Tower. By George Baird; Berlin, Germany; p. 193.

1981

Domus

Lyons Tower, Five Island Lake, Nova Scotia; Milan, Italy; September, p. 34

Drawing and Photography Credits

DRAWING / MODEL CREDITS

Brian MacKay-Lyons
has composed and formatted all of the
drawings in this book

Stephen Blood
18, 19

Marc Cormier
70, 71, 72, 73

Trevor Davis
38, 39

Adam Fawkes
52

Charles Fawkes
31, 52, 92, 94

Gary Fields
40

Susan Fitzgerald
17, 21, 25, 29, 33, 34, 37, 43, 47, 55, 58, 65, 66, 68, 71, 78, 87, 91

Darryl Jonas
34, 56, 80, 81

Miro Krawczynski
92, 95

Lois Luke
48, 49

Brian MacKay-Lyons
27, 31, 37, 57, 93, 96, 99

Robert Meyer
14, 70, 71, 72, 73

Niall Savage
26, 44, 45, 50, 83, 100

Peter Spierenburg
40, 41

Talbot Sweetapple
36, 38, 39, 98, 99, 101

Bruno Weber
22, 23, 30, 51, 59, 60, 62, 67, 70, 71, 72, 73

Doug Wigle
61

PHOTOGRAPHY CREDITS

Brent Ash
10

Arthur Baxter
48, 49

Bob Benz
4

Nicole Delmage
cover, 8

Charles Fawkes
25, 27

Terry James
21

Ken Kam
46, 47, 50, 51, 52, 53, 95, 105

Brian MacKay-Lyons
4, 9, 11, 74, 75, 79

Chris Oxner
9

Chris Reardon
42, 43, 44, 45, 82

Craig Rubadoux
4, 22, 23

James Steeves ©
16, 17, 19, 20, 23, 24, 26, 27, 28, 29, 30, 31, 32, 33, 34, 35, 36, 38, 39, 54, 55, 56, 57, 58, 59, 60, 61, 62, 63, 64, 65, 66, 67, 68, 69, 70, 71, 72, 73, 76, 77, 82, 83, 84, 85, 86, 87, 88, 89, 90, 96, 119

Paul Toman
91, 93, 94, 97

Tom Yee
19

Contributors

ESMAIL BANIASSAD

Essy Baniassad is a professor of architecture at Dalhousie University's Faculty of Architecture and a past president of the Royal Architectural Institute of Canada. He conceived and initiated the present series of monographs during his term as Dean of Faculty and is currently the general editor for Tuns Press.

BRIAN CARTER

Brian Carter is an architect who has worked in practice most recently with Arup Associates in London. A Fellow of the Royal Society of Arts, he is currently Professor and Chairman of Architecture at the University of Michigan.

ALEX COLVILLE

Alex Colville is a painter who lives and works in Wolfville, Nova Scotia. He is among Canada's most respected 20th century artists.

Acknowledgements

Maud Lewis Memorial 1997, Marshalltown, N.S.
Material: galvanized steel

Documents in Canadian Architecture is aimed at the 'student of architecture'. I am grateful for the opportunity to thank those who have contributed to 'the education of an architect'. That story begins with my father, Gerry Lyons, who inspired me as a child to follow a career in architecture and took me from Arcadia to Rome.

The role of the teacher is always critical. Had it not been for Larry Richards' belief in the value of design, I would not be an architect today. Historian Anthony Jackson gave me an appreciation for the importance of ideas. Jim Sykes has taught me a process view of architecture. These influences led me to Charles Moore – teacher, employer, colleague and friend – the complete architect as educator, practitioner and author, encompassed by his deep humanism. Essy Baniassad taught me to teach. The career of the painter, Alex Colville, is a model for practice outside of the mainstream.

The ultimate design project for the architect is the practice itself. Those that share the dreams and aspirations that make the heartaches worthwhile are soulmates: Attilio Gobbi, with his deep sense of history; Bob Benz, who taught me to see construction as design; my childhood friend, Michel Comeau, who shares a belief in the deep aesthetic link between structure and architecture; and Pat Langmaid, who has lent dignity to a struggling enterprise.

As in my own apprenticeship, my students have become colleagues and have made a contribution to the development of the work. It would take more than this page to acknowledge all of those students and graduates who have helped create the studio culture of the practice. However, a few stand out for their holistic impact on the practice: Michael Carroll, with his tough, Newfoundland outport mind; Niall Savage, who has lent his sense of style; John Geldart, who has applied his craft ethic; Talbot Sweetapple, the passionate designer; and Robert Meyer, with his low-brow intellectual toughness. These are instincts that I have come to rely on.

After graduation I realized, for survival, that architecture is a social art. Moore rejected the view of the architect as misunderstood genius, in favour of eliciting the energy of clients and users in a truly participatory process. Without creative and intellectually engaged clients, there would be no book. Similarly, I have developed a deep respect for builders as creative partners, who have taught me about material culture. G. Stewart MacKay's democratic values have inspired this daily practice.

It is Brian Carter's long-term interest and support for my work and consummate professionalism, the guiding vision of Essy Baniassad and the craftsmanship of Donald Westin that have made this project happen.

I have been fortunate to have a family that have unconditionally supported my career, and who have been willing to live in an architectural experiment with very intangible rewards. This book is dedicated to Marilyn, Renee, Alison and Matthew.

BML

rds for Architecture, ISBN 0-929112-38-5, 1997

tt & Company, ISBN 0-929112-31-8, 1996

29112-28-8, 1994

, Nova Scotia, ISBN 0-929112-19-9, 1993